𝕽𝖎𝖛𝖊𝖗𝖇𝖞 𝕰𝖉𝖎𝖙𝖎𝖔𝖓

THE WRITINGS OF
JOHN BURROUGHS

WITH PORTRAITS AND MANY ILLUSTRATIONS

VOLUME VIII

Clifton Johnson

THE WRITINGS

OF

JOHN BURROUGHS

VIII

INDOOR STUDIES

BOSTON AND NEW YORK

HOUGHTON MIFFLIN COMPANY

The Riverside Press, Cambridge

CONTENTS

LIST OF ILLUSTRATIONS

INDOOR STUDIES

INDOOR STUDIES

I

HENRY D. THOREAU

IN "Walden" Thoreau enumerates, in a serio-humorous vein, his various unpaid occupations, such as inspector of storms, surveyor of forest paths and all across-lot routes, shepherd and herder to the wild stock of the town, etc. Among the rest he says: "For a long time I was reporter to a journal of no very wide circulation, whose editor has never yet seen fit to print the bulk of my contributions, and, as is too common with writers, I got only my labor for my pains. However, in this case my pains were their own reward." The journal to which Thoreau so playfully alludes, consisting of many manuscript volumes, is now the property of Mr. H. G. O. Blake, an old friend and correspondent of his, and his rejected contributions to it, after a delay of nearly twenty years, are being put into print. "Early Spring in Massachusetts," "Summer," and "Winter," lately published, are made up of excerpts from this journal. A few of the passages in the former have been in print before. I notice one in the "Week," one or more in his discourse on "Walking, or the Wild," and one in the essay called "Life without Principle."

Thoreau published but two volumes in his lifetime, "A Week on the Concord and Merrimack Rivers" — which, by the way, is mainly a record of other and much longer voyages upon other and less tangible rivers than those named in the title — and "Walden, or Life in the Woods." The other six volumes of his works, including Mr. Blake's, have been collected and published since his death.[1]

Of Thoreau's journal as published by Mr. Blake I think it may be said that a good deal of it is evidently experimental with the author. There is often an attempt to make something out of nothing by the mere force of words. He squeezes his subject as in a vice ; we feel the effort he makes, but the result is often not worth the labor ; the precious drop he is after is not forthcoming. In fact, his journal is largely the record of a search for something he never fully finds: any fact of natural history or botany or geology which he does find is only incidental; he turns it over curiously, remarks upon it, and passes on in his chase of the unattainable. Yet there is most excellent and characteristic matter in his journal, and many valuable and

---

[1] Since this was written a new *Riverside Edition* of Thoreau's writings has been published in eleven volumes, including *Autumn*, from his journal, and a selection of his *Familiar Letters*.

Site of Thoreau's Hut

interesting natural history notes. When he wrote a book or a lecture or an essay, we are told, he went to his journal for the greater share of his material. He revised and corrected and supplemented his record from day to day and from year to year, till it often reflects truly his life and mind. He was a man so thoroughly devoted to principle and to his own aims in life that he seems never to have allowed himself one indifferent or careless moment. He was always making the highest demands upon himself and upon others.

In his private letters his bow is strung just as taut as in his printed works, and he uses arrows from the same quiver, and sends them just as high and far as he can. In his journal it appears to be the same.

Thoreau's fame has steadily increased since his death, in 1862, as it was bound to do. It was little more than in the bud at that time, and its full leaf and flowering are not yet, perhaps not in many years yet. He improves with age; in fact, requires age to take off a little of his asperity and fully ripen him. The generation he lectured so sharply will not give the same heed to his words as will the next and the next. The first effect of the reading of his books, upon many minds, is irritation and disapproval ; the perception of their beauty and wisdom comes later. He makes short work of our prejudices ; he likes the wind in his teeth, and to put it in the teeth of his reader. He was a man devoid of compassion, devoid of sympathy, devoid of generosity, devoid of patriotism, as these words are usually understood, yet his life showed a devotion to principle such as one life in millions does not show; and matching this there runs through his works a vein of the purest and rarest poetry and the finest wisdom. For both these reasons, time will enhance rather than lessen the value of his contributions. The world likes a good hater and refuser almost as well as it likes a good lover and acceptor, only it likes him farther off.

In writing of Thoreau, I am not conscious of having any criticism to make of him. I would fain accept him just as he was, and make the most of him, defining and discriminating him as I would a flower or a bird or any other product of nature, — perhaps exaggerating some features the better to bring them out. There were greater men among his contemporaries, but I doubt if there were any more genuine and sincere, or more devoted to ideal ends. If he was not this, that, or the other great man, he was Thoreau, and he fills his own niche well, and has left a positive and distinct impression upon the literature of his country. He did his work thoroughly; he touched bottom; he made the most of his life. He said: "I would not be one of those who will foolishly drive a nail into mere lath and plastering;" he would beat about with his hammer till he found the studding, and no one can study his life and books and not feel that he really drove his nail home into good solid timber. He was, perhaps, a little too near his friend and master, Emerson, and brought too directly under his influence. If he had lived farther from him, he would have felt his attraction less. But he was just as positive a fact as Emerson. The contour of his moral nature was just as firm and resisting. He was no more a soft-shelled egg, to be dented by every straw in the nest, than was his distinguished neighbor.

An English reviewer has summed up his estimate of Thoreau by calling him a "skulker," which is the pith of Dr. Johnson's smart epigram about Cowley, a man in whom Thoreau is distinctly foreshadowed: "If his activity was virtue, his retreat was cowardice." Thoreau was a skulker if it appears that he ran away from a noble part to perform an ignoble, or one less noble. The world has a right to the best there is in a man, both in word and deed, — from the scholar, knowledge; from the soldier, courage; from the statesman, wisdom; from the farmer, good husbandry, and from all, virtue: but has it a right to say arbitrarily who shall be soldiers and who poets? Is there no virtue but virtue? no religion but in the creeds? no salt but what is crystallized? Who shall presume to say the world did not get the best there was in Thoreau,

— high and much-needed service from him, — albeit there appear in the account more kicks than compliments? Would you have had him stick to his lead-pencils, or to school-teaching, and let Walden Pond and the rest go? We should have lost some of the raciest and most antiseptic books in English literature, and an example of devotion to principle that provokes and stimulates like a winter morning. I am not aware that Thoreau shirked any responsibility or dodged any duty proper to him, and he could look the world as squarely in the face as any man that ever lived.

The people of his native town remember at least one notable occasion on which Thoreau did not skulk, nor sulk either. I refer to the 30th of October, 1859, when he made his plea for Captain John Brown, while the hero was on trial in Virginia. It was proposed to stop Thoreau's mouth, persuade him to keep still and lie low, but he was not to be stopped. He thought there were enough lying low, — the ranks were all full there, the ground was covered; and in an address delivered in Concord he glorified the old hero in words that, at this day and in the light of subsequent events, it thrills the blood to read. This instant and unequivocal indorsement of John Brown by Thoreau, in the face of the most overwhelming public opinion even among anti-slavery men, throws a flood of light upon him. It is the most significant act of his life. It clinches him;

it makes the colors fast. We know he means what he says after that. It is of the same metal and has the same ring as John Brown's act itself. It shows what thoughts he had fed his soul on, what school he had schooled himself in, what his devotion to the ideal meant. His hatred of slavery and injustice, and of the government that tolerated them, was pure, and it went clean through; it stopped at nothing. Iniquitous laws must be defied, and there is no previous question. "The fact that the politician fears," he says, referring to the repeal of the Fugitive Slave Law, "is merely that there is less honor among thieves than was supposed, and not the fact that they are thieves." For the most part, Thoreau's political tracts and addresses seem a little petulant and willful, and fall just short of enlisting one's sympathies; and his carrying his opposition to the state to the point of allowing himself to be put in jail rather than pay a paltry tax, savors a little bit of the grotesque and the melodramatic. But his plea for John Brown when the whole country was disowning him, abolitionists and all, fully satisfies one's sense of the fitness of things. It does not overshoot the mark. The mark was high, and the attitude of the speaker was high and scornful, and uncompromising in the extreme. It was just the occasion required to show Thoreau's metal. "If this man's acts and words do not create a revival, it will be the severest possible satire on the acts and words that do. It is the best news that America has ever heard." "Think of him, — of his rare qualities! — such a man as it takes ages to make, and ages to understand; no mock hero, nor the representative of any party. A man such as the sun may not rise upon again in this benighted land, to whose making went the costliest material, the finest adamant; sent to be the redeemer of those in captivity; and the only use to which you can put him is to hang him at the end of a rope!" "Do yourselves the honor to recognize him; he needs none of your respect." It was just such radical qualities as John Brown exhibited, or their analogue and counterpart in other fields, that Thoreau coveted and pursued through life: in man, devotion to the severest ideal, friendship founded upon antagonism, or hate, as he preferred to call it; in nature, the untamed and untamable, even verging on the savage and pitiless; in literature, the heroic, — "books, not which afford us a cowering enjoyment, but in which each thought is of unusual daring; such as an idle man cannot read, and a timid one would not be entertained by." Indeed, Thoreau was Brown's spiritual brother, the last and finer flowering of the same plant, — the seed flowering; he was just as much of a zealot, was just as gritty and unflinching in his way; a man whose brow was set, whose mind was made up, and leading just as forlorn a hope, and as little quailed by the odds.

HENRY D. THOREAU

In the great army of Mammon, the great army of the fashionable, the complacent and church-going, Thoreau was a skulker, even a deserter, if you please, — yea, a traitor fighting on the other side.

Emerson regrets the loss to the world of his rare powers of action, and thinks that, instead of being the captain of a huckleberry-party, he might have engineered for all America. But Thoreau, doubt-less, knew himself better when he said, with his usual strength of metaphor, that he was as unfit for the coarse uses of this world as gossamer for ship-timber. A man who believes that "life should be lived as tenderly and daintily as one would pluck a flower," and actually and seriously aims to live his life so, is not a man to engineer for all America. If you want a columbiad, you must have tons and tons of gross metal; and if you want an engineer for all America, leader and wielder of vast masses of men, you must have a certain breadth and coarse-ness of fibre in your hero: but if you want a trench-ant blade like Thoreau, you must leave the pot-metal out and look for something bluer and finer.

Thoreau makes a frank confession upon this very point in his journal, written when he was but twenty-five. "I must confess I have felt mean enough when asked how I was to act on society, what errand I had to mankind. Undoubtedly I did not feel mean without a reason, and yet my loitering is not without a defense. I would fain communicate the wealth of my life to men, would really give them what is most precious in my gift. I would secrete pearls with the shellfish, and lay up honey with the bees for them. I will sift the sunbeams for the public good. I know no riches I would keep back." And his subsequent life made good these words. He gave the world the strongest and bravest there was in him, the pearls of his life, — not a fat oyster, not a reputation unctuous with benevolence and easy good-will, but a character crisp and pearl-like, full of hard, severe words and stimulating taunts and demands. Thoreau was an extreme product, an extreme type of mind and character, and was naturally more or less isolated from his surroundings. He planted himself far beyond the coast-line that bounds most lives, and seems insular and solitary; but he believed he had the granite floor of principle beneath him, and without the customary intervening clay or quicksands.

Of a profile we say the outlines are strong, or they are weak and broken. The outlines of Thoreau's moral nature are strong and noble, but the direct face-to-face expression of his character is not always pleasing, not always human. He appears best in profile, when looking away from you and not toward you, — when looking at nature and not at man. He combined a remarkable strength of will with a nature singularly sensitive and delicate, — the most fair and fragile of wood-flowers on an iron stem. With more freedom and flexibility of character, greater capacity for self-surrender and self-abandonment, he would have been a great poet. But his principal aim in life was moral and intellectual, rather than artistic. He was an ascetic before he was a poet, and he cuts the deepest in the direction of character and conduct. He had no caution or prudence in the ordinary sense, no worldly temporizing qualities of any kind; was impatient of the dross and alloy of life, — would have it pure flame, pure purpose and aspiration; and, so far as he could make it, his life was so. He was, by nature, of the Opposition; he had a constitutional No in him that could not be tortured into Yes. He was of the stuff that saints and martyrs and devotees, or, if you please, fanatics are made of, and no doubt, in an earlier age, would have faced the rack or the stake with perfect composure. Such a man is bound to make an impression by contrast, if not by comparison, with the men of his country and time. He is, for the most part, a figure going the other way from that of the eager, money-getting, ambitious crowd, and he questions and admonishes and ridicules the passers-by sharply. We all see him and remember him, and feel his shafts. Especially was his attitude upon all social and political questions scornful and exasperating. His devotion to principle, to the ideal, was absolute; it was like that of the Hindu to his idol. If it devoured him or crushed him, — what business was that of his? There was no conceivable failure in adherence to principle.

Thoreau was, probably, the wildest civilized man this country has produced, adding to the shyness of the hermit and woodsman the wildness of the poet, and to the wildness of the poet the greater ferity and elusiveness of the mystic. An extreme product of civilization and of modern culture, he was yet as untouched by the worldly and commercial spirit of his age and country as any red man that ever haunted the shores of his native stream. He put the whole of nature between himself and his fellows. A man of the strongest local attachments, — not the least nomadic, seldom wandering beyond his native township, — yet his spirit was as restless and as impatient of restraint as any nomad or Tartar that ever lived. He cultivated an extreme wildness, not only in his pursuits and tastes, but in his hopes and imaginings. He says to his friend, "Hold fast your most indefinite waking dream." Emerson says his life was an attempt to pluck the Swiss edelweiss from the all but inaccessible cliffs. The higher and the wilder, the more the fascination for him. Indeed, the loon, the moose, the beaver, were but faint types and symbols of the wildness he coveted and would have reappear in his life and books; not the cosmical, the universal, — he was not great enough for that, — but simply the wild as distinguished from the domestic and the familiar, the remote and the surprising as contrasted with the hackneyed and the commonplace, arrow-heads as distinguished from whetstones or jackknives.

Thoreau was French on one side and Puritan on the other. It was probably the wild, untamable French core in him — a dash of the gray wolf that stalks through his ancestral folk-lore, as in Audubon and the Canadian *voyageurs* — that made him turn with such zest and such genius to aboriginal nature; and it was the Puritan element in him — strong, grim, uncompromising, almost heartless — that held him to such high, austere, moral, and ideal ends. His genius was Saxon in its homeliness and sincerity, in its directness and scorn of rhetoric; but that wild revolutionary cry of his, and that sort of restrained ferocity and hirsuteness, are more French. He said in one of his letters, when he was but twenty-four: "I grow savager and savager every day, as if fed on raw meat, and my tameness is only the repose of untamableness." But his savageness took a mild form. He could not even eat meat; it was unclean and offended his imagination, and when he went to Maine, he felt for weeks that his nature had been made the coarser because he had witnessed the killing of a moose. His boasted savageness, the gray wolf in him, only gave a more decided grit or grain to his mental and moral nature, — made him shut his teeth the more firmly, sometimes even with an audible snap and growl, upon the poor lambs and ewes and superannuated wethers of the social, religious, and political folds.

In his moral and intellectual growth and experience, Thoreau seems to have reacted strongly from a marked tendency to invalidism in his own body. He would be well in spirit at all hazards. What was this never-ending search of his for the wild but a search for health, for something tonic and antiseptic in nature? Health, health, give me health, is his cry. He went forth into nature as the boys go to the fields and woods in spring after wintergreens, black birch, crinkle-root, and sweet-flag; he had an unappeasable hunger for the pungent, the aromatic, the bitter-sweet, for the very rind and salt of the globe. He fairly gnaws the ground and the trees in his walk, so craving is his appetite for the wild. He went to Walden to study, but it was as a deer goes to a deer-lick; the brine he was after did abound there. Any trait of wildness and freedom suddenly breaking out in any of the domestic animals, as when your cow leaped your fence like a deer and ate up your corn, or your horse forgot that he was not a mustang on the plains, and took the bit in his teeth, and left your buggy and family behind high and dry, etc., was eagerly snapped up by him. Ah, you have not tamed them, you have not broken them yet! He makes a most charming entry in his journal about a little boy he one day saw in the street, with a home-made cap on his head made of a woodchuck's skin. He seized upon it as a horse with the crib-bite seizes upon a post. It tasted good to him.

"The great gray-tipped hairs were all preserved, and stood out above the brown ones, only a little more loosely than in life. It was as if he had put his head into the belly of a woodchuck, having cut off his tail and legs, and substituted a visor for the head. The little fellow wore it innocently enough, not knowing what he had on forsooth, going about his small business pit-a-pat, and his black eyes sparkled beneath it when I remarked on its warmth, even as the woodchuck's might have done. Such should be the history of every piece of clothing that we wear."

He says how rarely are we encouraged by the sight of simple actions in the street; but when one day he saw an Irishman wheeling home from far a large, damp, and rotten pine log for fuel, he felt encouraged. That looked like fuel; it warmed him to think of it. The piles of solid oak-wood which he saw in other yards did not interest him at all in comparison. It savored of the wild, and, though water-soaked, his fancy kindled at the sight.

He loved wild men, not tame ones. Any half-wild Irishman, or fisherman, or hunter in his neighborhood he was sure to get a taste of sooner or later. He seems to have had a hankering for the Indian all his life; could eat him raw, one would think. In fact, he did try him when he went to Maine, and succeeded in extracting more nutriment out of him than any other man has done. He found him rather tough diet, and was probably a little disappointed in him, but he got something out of him akin to that which the red squirrel gets out of a pine-cone. In his books he casts many a longing and envious glance upon the Indian. Some old Concord sachem seems to have looked into his fount of life and left his image there. His annual spring search for arrow-heads was the visible outcropping of this aboriginal trace. How he prized these relics! One is surprised to see how much he gets out of them. They become arrow-root instead of arrow-stones. "They are sown, like a grain that is slow to germinate, broadcast over the earth. As the dragon's teeth bore a crop of soldiers, so these bear crops of philosophers and poets, and the same seed is just as good to plant again. It is a stone-fruit. Each one yields me a thought. I come nearer to the maker of it than if I found his bones." "When I see these signs, I know that the subtle spirits that made them are not far off, into whatever form transmuted."[1] Our poetry, he said, was white man's poetry, and he longed to hear what the Indian muse had to say. I think he liked the Indian's paint and feathers. Certainly he did his skins, and the claws and hooked beaks with which

[1] *Early Spring in Massachusetts*, pp. 259, 260.

he adorned himself. He puts a threatening claw or beak into his paragraphs whenever he can, and feathers his shafts with the nicest art.

So wild a man, and such a lover of the wild, and yet it does not appear that he ever sowed any wild oats. Though he somewhere exclaims impatiently, "What demon possesses me that I behave so well?" he took it all out in transcendentalism and arrow-heads. His only escapades were eloping with a mountain or coquetting with Walden Pond! He sees a water-bug, and at once exclaims, "Ah! if I had no more sins to answer for than a water-bug!" Had he any more? His weakness was that he had no weakness, — it was only unkindness. He had a deeper centre-board than most men, and he carried less sail. The passions and emotions and ambitions of his fellows, which are sails that so often need to be close-reefed and double-reefed, he was quite free from. Thoreau's isolation, his avoidance of the world, was in self-defense, no doubt. His genius would not bear the contact of rough hands any more than would butterflies' wings. He says in "Walden:" "The finest qualities of our nature, like the bloom on fruits, can be preserved only by the most delicate handling." This bloom, this natural innocence, Thoreau was very jealous of and sought to keep unimpaired, and, perhaps, succeeded as few men ever have. He says you cannot even know evil without being a *parti-*

ceps criminis. He did not so much regret the condition of things in this country (in 1861) as that he had ever heard of it.

Yet Thoreau creates as much consternation among the saints as among the sinners. His delicacy and fineness were saved by a kind of cross-grain there was in him, — a natural twist and stubbornness of fibre. He was not easily reduced to kindling-wood. His self-indulgences were other men's crosses. His attitude was always one of resistance and urge. He hated sloth and indolence and compliance as he hated rust. He thought nothing was so much to be feared as fear, and that atheism might, comparatively, be popular with God himself. Beware even the luxury of affection, he says, — "There must be some nerve and heroism in our love, as in a winter morning." He tells his correspondent to make his failure tragical by the earnestness and steadfastness of his endeavor, and then it will not differ from success. His saintliness is a rock-crystal. He says in "Walden:" "Probably I should not consciously and deliberately forsake my particular calling to do the good which society demands of me, to save the universe from annihilation; and I believe that a like but infinitely greater steadfastness elsewhere is all that now preserves it." Is this crystal a diamond? What will it not cut?

There is no grain of concession or compromise in this man. He asks no odds and he pays no boot.

He will have his way, but his way is not down the stream with the current. He loves to warp up it against wind and tide, holding fast by his anchor at night. When he is chagrined or disgusted, it convinces him his health is better, — that there is some vitality left. It is not compliments his friends get from him, — rather taunts. The caress of the hand may be good, but the sting of its palm is good also. No is more bracing and tonic than Yes. He said: "I love to go through a patch of scrub-oaks in a bee-line, — where you tear your clothes and put your eyes out." The spirit of antagonism never sleeps with Thoreau, and the love of paradox is one of his guiding stars. "The longer I have forgotten you, the more I remember you," he says to his correspondent. "My friend is cold and reserved, because his love for me is waxing and not waning," he says in his journal. The difficult and the disagreeable are in the line of his self-indulgence. Even lightning will choose the easiest way out of the house, — an open window or door. Thoreau would rather go through the solid wall, or mine out through the cellar.

When he is sad, his only regret is that he is not sadder. He says if his sadness were only sadder, it would make him happier. In writing to his friend, he says it is not sad to him to hear she has sad hours: "I rather rejoice in the richness of your experience." In one of his letters, he charges his correspondent to "improve every opportunity to be melancholy," and accuses himself of being too easily contented with a slight and almost animal happiness. "My happiness is a good deal like that of the woodchucks." He says that "of acute sorrow I suppose that I know comparatively little. My saddest and most genuine sorrows are apt to be but transient regrets." Yet he had not long before lost by death his brother John, with whom he made his voyage on the Concord and Merrimack. Referring to John's death, he said: "I find these things more strange than sad to me. What right have I to grieve who have not ceased to wonder?" and says in effect, afterward, that any pure grief is its own reward. John, he said, he did not wish ever to see again, — not the John that was dead (O Henry! Henry!), John as he was in the flesh, but the ideal, the nobler John, of whom the real was the imperfect representative. When the son of his friend died, he wasted no human regrets. It seemed very natural and proper that he should die. "Do not the flowers die every autumn?" "His fine organization demanded it [death], and nature gently yielded its request. It would have been strange if he had lived."

Either Thoreau was destitute of pity and love (in the human sense), and of many other traits that are thought to be both human and divine, or else he studiously suppressed them and thought them

unworthy of him. He writes and talks a great deal
about love and friendship, and often with singular
beauty and appreciation, yet he always says to his
friend: "Stand off — keep away! Let there be an
unfathomable gulf between us, — let there be a
wholesome hate." Indeed, love and hatred seem
inseparable in his mind, and curiously identical.
He writes in his journal that "words should pass
between friends as the lightning passes from cloud
to cloud." One of his poems begins: —

> "Let such pure hate still underprop
> Our love, that we may be
> Each other's conscience,
> And have our sympathy
> Mainly from thence.

> "Surely, surely, thou wilt trust me
> When I say thou dost disgust me.
> Oh, I hate thee with a hate
> That would fain annihilate;
> Yet, sometimes, against my will,
> My dear friend, I love thee still.
> It were treason to our love,
> And a sin to God above,
> One iota to abate
> Of a pure, impartial hate."

This is the salt with which he seasons and preserves his love, — hatred. In this pickle it will
keep. Without it, it would become stale and vulgar.

Good-nature and conciliation were not among his accomplishments, and yet he puts his reader in a genial and happy frame of mind. He is the occasion of unction and heartiness in others, if he has not them in himself. He says of himself, with great penetration: "My only integral experience is in my vision. I see, perchance, with more integrity than I feel." His sympathies lead you into narrow quarters, but his vision takes you to the hill-tops. As regards humanity and all that goes with it, he was like an inverted cone, and grew broader and broader the farther he got from it. He approached things, or even men, but very little through his humanity or his manliness. How delightful his account of the Canadian wood-chopper in "Walden," and yet he sees him afar off, across an impassable gulf! — he is a kind of Homeric or Paphlagonian man to him. Very likely he would not have seen him at all had it not been for the classic models and ideals with which his mind was filled, and which saw for him.

Yet Thoreau doubtless liked the flavor of strong, racy men. He said he was naturally no hermit, but ready enough to fasten himself, like a bloodsucker for the time, to any full-blooded man that came in his way; and he gave proof of this when he saw and recognized the new poet, Walt Whitman. Here is the greatest democrat the world has seen, he said, and he found him exhilarating and encouraging, while yet he felt somewhat imposed upon by his heartiness and broad generalities. As a writer, Thoreau shows all he is, and more. Nothing is kept back; greater men have had far less power of statement. His thoughts do not merely crop out, but lie upon the surface of his pages. They are fragments; there is no more than you see. It is not the edge or crown of the native rock, but a drift boulder. He sees clearly, thinks swiftly, and the sharp emphasis and decision of his mind strew his pages with definite and striking images and ideas. His expression is never sod-bound, and you get its full force at once.

One of his chief weapons is a kind of restrained extravagance of statement, a compressed exaggeration of metaphor. The hyperbole is big, but it is gritty, and is firmly held. Sometimes it takes the form of paradox, as when he tells his friend that he needs his hate as much as his love: —

> "Indeed, indeed, I cannot tell,
> Though I ponder on it well,
> Which were easier to state,
> All my love or all my hate."

Or when he says, in "Walden:" "Our manners have been corrupted by communication with the saints," and the like. Sometimes it becomes downright brag, as when he says, emphasizing his own preoccupation and indifference to events: "I would not run around the corner to see the world blow up;" or again: "Methinks I would hear with indifference if a trustworthy messenger were to inform me that the sun drowned himself last night." Again it takes an impish ironical form, as when he says: "In heaven I hope to bake my own bread and clean my own linen." Another time it assumes a half-quizzical, half-humorous turn, as when he tells one of his correspondents that he was so warmed up in getting his winter's wood that he considered, after he got it housed, whether he should not dispose of it to the ash-man, as if he had extracted all its heat. Often it gives only an added emphasis to his expression, as when he says: "A little thought is sexton to all the world;" or, "Some circumstantial evidence is very strong, as when you find a trout in the milk;" but its best and most constant office is to act as a kind of fermenting, expanding gas that lightens, if it sometimes inflates, his page. His exaggeration is saved by its wit, its unexpectedness. It gives a wholesome jostle and shock to the mind.

Thoreau was not a racy writer, but a trenchant; not nourishing so much as stimulating; not convincing, but wholesomely exasperating and arousing, which, in some respects, is better. There is no heat in him, and yet in reading him one understands what he means when he says that, sitting by his stove at night, he sometimes had thoughts that kept the fire warm. I think the mind of his reader always reacts healthfully and vigorously from his most rash and extreme statements. The blood comes to the surface and to the extremities with a bound. He is the best of counter-irritants when he is nothing else. There is nothing to reduce the tone of your moral and intellectual systems in Thoreau. Such heat as there is in refrigeration, as he himself might say, — you are always sure of that in his books.

His literary art, like that of Emerson, is in the unexpected turn of his sentences. Shakespeare says: —

> "It is the witness still of excellency
> To put a strange face on his own perfection."

This "strange face" Thoreau would have at all hazards, even if it was a false face. If he could not state a truth he would state a paradox, which, however, is not always a false face. He must make the commonest facts and occurrences wear a strange and unfamiliar look. The commonplace he would give a new dress, even if he set it masquerading. But the reader is always the gainer by this tendency in him. It gives a fresh and novel coloring to what in other writers would prove flat and wearisome. He made the whole world interested in his private experiment at Walden Pond by the strange and, on the whole, beaming face he put upon it. Of course, this is always more or less the art of genius, but it was preëminently the art of Thoreau. We are not buoyed up by great power, we do not swim lightly as in deep water, but we are amused and stimulated, and now and then positively electrified.

To make an extreme statement, and so be sure that he made an emphatic one, that was his aim. Exaggeration is less to be feared than dullness and tameness. The far-fetched is good if you fetch it swift enough ; you must make its heels crack, — jerk it out of its boots, in fact. Cushions are good, provided they are well stuck with pins ; you will be sure not to go to sleep in that case. Warm your benumbed hands in the snow; that is a more wholesome warmth than that of the kitchen stove. This is the way he underscored his teachings. Sometimes he racked his bones to say the unsayable. His mind had a strong gripe, and he often brings a great pressure to bear upon the most vague and subtle problems, or shadows of problems, but he never quite succeeds to my satisfaction in condensing bluing from the air or from the Indian summer haze, any more than he succeeded in extracting health and longevity from water-gruel and rye-meal.

He knew what an exaggeration he was, and he went about it deliberately. He says to one of his correspondents, a Mr. B——, whom he seems to have delighted to pummel with these huge boxing-gloves: "I trust that you realize what an exaggerator I am, — that I lay myself out to exaggerate whenever I have an opportunity, — pile Pelion upon Ossa to reach heaven so. Expect no trivial truth from me, unless I am on the witness-stand. I will come as near to lying as you can drive a coach-and-four."

We have every reason to be thankful that he was not always or commonly on the witness-stand. The record would have been much duller. Eliminate from him all his exaggerations, all his magnifying of the little, all his inflation of bubbles, etc., and you make sad havoc in his pages, — as you would, in fact, in any man's. Of course, it is one thing to bring the distant near, and thus magnify as does the telescope, and it is quite another thing to inflate a pigmy to the stature of a giant with a gaspipe. But Thoreau brings the stars as near as any writer I know of, and if he sometimes magnifies a will-o'-the-wisp, too, what matters it? He had a hard common sense, as well as an uncommon sense, and he knows well when he is conducting you to the brink of one of his astonishing hyperboles, and inviting you to take the leap with him, and, what is more, he knows that you know it. Nobody is deceived, and the game is well played. Writing to a correspondent who had been doing some big mountain-climbing, he says: —

"It is after we get home that we really go over the mountain, if ever. What did the mountain say? What did the mountain do? I keep a mountain anchored off eastward a little way, which I ascend in my dreams, both awake and asleep. Its broad base spreads over a village or two, which do not know it; neither does it know them, nor do I when I ascend it. I can see its general outline as plainly now in my mind as that of Wachusett. I do not invent in the least, but state exactly what I see. I find that I go up it when I am light-footed and earnest. I am not aware that a single villager frequents it, or knows of it. I keep this mountain to ride instead of a horse." What a saving clause is that last one, and what humor!

The bird Thoreau most admired was Chanticleer, crowing from his perch in the morning. He says the merit of that strain is its freedom from all plaintiveness. Unless our philosophy hears the cockcrow in the morning, it is belated. "It is an expression of the health and soundness of Nature, — a brag for all the world." "Who has not betrayed his Master many times since he last heard that note?" "The singer can easily move us to tears or to laughter, but where is he who can excite in us a pure morning joy? When in doleful dumps, breaking the awful stillness of our wooden sidewalk on a Sunday, or perchance a watcher in the house of mourning, I hear a cockerel crow, far or near, I think to myself, 'There is one of us well at any rate,' and with a sudden gush return to my senses."

Thoreau pitched his "Walden" in this key; he claps his wings and gives forth a clear, saucy, cheery, triumphant note, — if only to wake his neighbors up. And the book is certainly the most delicious piece of brag in literature. There is nothing else like it ; nothing so good, certainly. It is a challenge and a triumph, and has a morning freshness and *élan*. Read the chapter on his "bean-field." One wants to go forthwith and plant a field with beans, and hoe them barefoot. It is a kind of celestial agriculture. "When my hoe tinkled against the stones, that music echoed to the woods and the sky, and was an accompaniment to my labor which yielded an instant and immeasurable crop. It was no longer beans that I hoed, nor I that hoed beans; and I remembered with as much pity as pride, if I remembered at all, my acquaintances who had gone to the city to attend the oratorios." "On gala days the town fires its great guns, which echo like pop-guns to these woods, and some waif of martial music occasionally penetrated thus far. To me, away there in my bean-field and the other end of the town, the big guns sounded as if a puff-ball had burst; and when there was a military turn-out of which I was ignorant, I have sometimes had a vague sense all day, — of some sort of itching and disease in the horizon, as if some eruption would break out there soon, either scarlatina or canker-rash, — until at length some more favorable puff of wind, making haste over the fields and up the Wayland road, brought me information of the 'trainers'!"

What visitors he had, too, in his little hut — what royal company! — "especially in the morning, when nobody called." "One inconvenience I sometimes experience in so small a house, — the difficulty of getting to a sufficient distance from my guest when we began to utter the big thoughts in big words." "The bullet of your thought must have overcome its lateral and ricochet motion and fallen into its last and steady course before it reaches the ear of the hearer, else it may plow out again through the side of his head." He bragged that Concord could show him nearly everything worth seeing in the world or in nature; and that he did not need to read Dr. Kane's "Arctic Voyages" for phenomena that he could observe at home. He declined all invitations to go abroad, because he should then lose so much of Concord. As much of Paris, or London, or Berlin as he got, so much of Concord should he lose. He says in his journal: "It would be a wretched bargain to accept the proudest Paris in exchange for my native village." "At best, Paris could only be a school in which to learn to live here, — a stepping-stone to Concord, a school

Site of Thoreau's Beanfield

in which to fit for this university." "The sight of a marsh-hawk in Concord meadows is worth more to me than the entry of the Allies into Paris." This is very Parisian and Victor Hugoish, except for its self-consciousness and the playful twinkle in the author's eye.

Thoreau had humor, but it had worked a little, — it was not quite sweet; a vinous fermentation had taken place more or less in it. There was too much acid for the sugar. It shows itself especially when he speaks of men. How he disliked the average social and business man, and said his only resource was to get away from them! He was surprised to find what vulgar fellows they were. "They do a little business commonly each day, in order to pay their board, and then they congregate in sitting-rooms, and feebly fabulate and paddle in the social slush; and when I think that they have sufficiently relaxed, and am prepared to see them steal away to their shrines, they go unashamed to their beds, and take on a new layer of sloth." Methinks there is a drop of aquafortis in this liquor. Generally, however, there is only a pleasant acid or sub-acid flavor to his humor, as when he refers to a certain minister who spoke of God as if he enjoyed a monopoly of the subject; or when he says of the good church-people that "they show the whites of their eyes on the Sabbath, and the blacks all the rest of the week." He says the greatest bores who visited him in his hut by Walden Pond were the self-styled reformers, who thought that he was forever singing, —

> "This is the house that I built;
> This is the man that lives in the house that I built.

But they did not know that the third line was, —

> These are the folks that worry the man
> That lives in the house that I built.

I did not fear the hen-harriers, for I kept no chickens, but I feared the men-harriers rather."

What sweet and serious humor in that passage in "Walden" wherein he protests that he was not lonely in his hermitage: —

"I have occasional visits in the long winter evenings, when the snow falls fast and the wind howls in the wood, from an old settler and original proprietor, who is reported to have dug Walden Pond and stoned it, and fringed it with pine-woods; who tells me stories of old time and of new eternity; and between us we manage to pass a cheerful evening with social mirth and pleasant views of things, even without apples or cider, — a most wise and humorous friend, whom I love much, who keeps himself more secret than ever did Goffe or Whalley; and though he is thought to be dead, none can show where he is buried. An elderly dame, too, dwells in my neighborhood, invisible to most persons, in whose odorous herb-garden I love to stroll sometimes, gathering simples and listening to her fables; for she has a genius of unequaled fertility, and her memory runs back farther than mythology, and she can tell me the original of every fable, and on what fact every one is founded, for the incidents occurred when she was young. A ruddy and lusty old dame, who delights in all weathers and seasons, and is likely to outlive all her children yet."

Emerson says Thoreau's determination on natural history was organic, but it was his determination on supernatural history that was organic. Natural history was but one of the doors through which he sought to gain admittance to this inner and finer heaven of things. He hesitated to call himself a naturalist; probably even poet-naturalist would not have suited him. He says in his journal: "The truth is, I am a mystic, a transcendentalist, and a natural philosopher to boot," and the least of these is the natural philosopher. He says: "Man cannot afford to be a naturalist, to look at Nature directly, but only with the side of his eye. He must look through and beyond her. To look at her is as fatal as to look at the head of Medusa. It turns the man of science to stone." It is not looking at Nature that turns the man of science to stone, but looking at his dried and labeled specimens, and his dried and labeled theories of her. Thoreau always sought to look through and beyond her, and he missed seeing much there was in her ; the jealous goddess had her revenge. I do not make this remark as a criticism, but to account for his failure to make any new or valuable contribution to natural history. He did not love Nature for her own sake, or the bird and the flower for their own sakes, or with an unmixed and disinterested love, as Gilbert White did, for instance, but for what he could make out of them. He says: "The ultimate expression or fruit of any created thing is a fine effluence which only the most ingenuous worshiper perceives at a reverent distance from its surface even." [1] This "fine effluence" he was always reaching after, and often grasping or inhaling. This is the mythical hound and horse and turtle-dove which he says in "Walden" he long ago lost, and has been on their trail ever since. He never abandons the search, and in every woodchuck-hole or muskrat den, in retreat of bird, or squirrel, or mouse, or fox that he pries into, in every walk and expedition to the fields or swamps or to distant woods, in every spring note and call that he listens to so patiently, he hopes to get some clew to his lost treasures, to the effluence that so provokingly eludes him.

Hence, when we regard Thoreau simply as an observer or as a natural historian, there have been better, though few so industrious and persistent. He was up and out at all hours of the day and

[1] *Early Spring in Massachusetts*, p. 83.

night, and in all seasons and weathers, year in and year out, and yet he saw and recorded nothing new. It is quite remarkable. He says in his journal that he walked half of each day, and kept it up perhaps for twenty years or more. Ten years of persistent spying and inspecting of nature, and no new thing found out; and so little reported that is in itself interesting, that is, apart from his description of it. I cannot say that there was any felicitous and happy seeing ; there was no inspiration of the eye, certainly not in the direction of natural history. He has added no new line or touch to the portrait of bird or beast that I can recall, — no important or significant fact to their lives. What he saw in this field everybody may see who looks; it is patent. He had not the detective eye of the great naturalist; he did not catch the clews and hints dropped here and there, the quick, flashing movements, the shy but significant gestures by which new facts are disclosed, mainly because he was not looking for them. His eye was not penetrating and interpretive. It was full of speculation; it was sophisticated with literature, sophisticated with Concord, sophisticated with himself. His mood was subjective rather than objective. He was more intent on the natural history of his own thought than on that of the bird. To the last, his ornithology was not quite sure, not quite trustworthy. In his published journal he sometimes names the wrong bird; and what short work a naturalist would have made of his night-warbler, which Emerson reports Thoreau had been twelve years trying to identify! It was perhaps his long-lost turtle-dove, in some one of its disguises. From his journal it would seem that he was a long time puzzled to distinguish the fox-colored sparrow from the tree or Canadian sparrow, — a very easy task to one who has an eye for the birds. But he was looking too intently for a bird behind the bird, — for a mythology to shine through his ornithology. "The song sparrow and the transient fox-colored sparrow, — have they brought me no message this year? Is not the coming of the fox-colored sparrow something more earnest and significant than I have dreamed of? Have I heard what this tiny passenger has to say while it flits thus from tree to tree?" "I love the birds and beasts because they are mythologically in earnest." [1]

If he had had the same eye for natural history that he possessed for arrow-heads, what new facts he would have disclosed! But he was looking for arrow-heads. He had them in his mind; he thought arrow-heads; he was an arrow-head himself, and these relics fairly kicked themselves free of the mould to catch his eye.

"It is surprising how thickly strewn our soil is with arrow-heads. I never see the surface broken in sandy places but I think of them. I find them

[1] *Early Spring in Massachusetts*, p. 286.

on all sides, not only in corn, grain, potato, and bean fields, but in pastures and woods, by wood-chucks' holes and pigeon beds, and, as to-night, in a pasture where a restless cow had pawed the ground."

Thoreau was a man eminently "preoccupied of his own soul." He had no self-abandonment, no self-forgetfulness; he could not give himself to the birds or animals: they must surrender to him. He says to one of his correspondents: "Whether he sleeps or wakes, whether he runs or walks, whether he uses a microscope or a telescope, or his naked eye, a man never discovers anything, never over-takes anything, or leaves anything behind, but him-self." This is half true of some; it is wholly true of others. It is wholly true of Thoreau. Nature was the glass in which he saw himself. He says the partridge loves peas, but not those that go into the pot with her! All the peas Thoreau loved had been in the pot with him and were seasoned by him.

I trust I do not in the least undervalue Thoreau's natural history notes; I only wish there were more of them. What makes them so valuable and charm-ing is his rare descriptive powers. He could give the simple fact with the freshest and finest poetic bloom upon it. If there is little or no felicitous seeing in Thoreau, there is felicitous description: he does not see what another would not, but he describes what he sees as few others can; his happy literary talent makes up for the poverty of his observation. That is, we are never surprised at what he sees, but are surprised and tickled at the way he tells what he sees. He notes, for instance, the arrival of the high-hole in spring; we all note it, every schoolboy notes it, but who has described it as Thoreau does : " The loud *peop* of a pigeon woodpecker is heard, and anon the prolonged loud and shrill cackle calling the thin-wooded hillsides and pastures to life. It is like the note of an alarm-clock set last fall so as to wake Nature up at exactly this date, — *up, up, up, up, up, up, up, up, up, up !*" He says: "The note of the first bluebird in the air answers to the purling rill of melted snow beneath. It is evidently soft and soothing, and, as surely as the thermometer, indicates a higher temperature. It is the accent of the south wind, its vernacular."

Often a single word or epithet of his tells the whole story. Thus he says, speaking of the music of the blackbird, that it has a "split-whistle;" the note of the red-shouldered starling is "gurgle-*ee*." Looking out of his window one March day, he says he cannot see the heel of a single snowbank anywhere. He does not seem to have known that the shrike sings in the fall and winter as well as in the spring ; and is he entirely sure he saw a muskrat building its house in March (the fall is the time they build); or that he heard the whip-poor-will singing in September; or that the woodchuck dines principally upon crickets? With what patience and industry he watched things for a sign! From his journal it would appear that Thoreau kept nature about Concord under a sort of police surveillance the year round. He shadowed every flower and bird and musquash that appeared. His vigilance was unceasing; not a mouse or a squirrel must leave its den without his knowledge. If the birds or frogs were not on hand promptly at his spring roll-call, he would know the reason; he would look them up; he would question his neighbors. He was up in the morning and off to some favorite haunt earlier than the day-laborers; and he chronicled his observations on the spot, as if the case was to be tried in court the next day and he was the principal witness. He watched the approach of spring as a doctor watches the development of a critical case. He felt the pulse of the wind and the temperature of the day at all hours. He examined the plants growing under water, and noted the radical leaves of various weeds that keep green all winter under the snow. He felt for them with benumbed fingers amid the wet and the snow. The first sight of bare ground and of the red earth excited him. The fresh meadow spring odor was to him like the fragrance of tea to an old tea-drinker. In early March he goes to the Corner Spring to see the tufts of green grass, or he inspects the minute lichens that spring from the bark of trees. "It is short commons," he says, "and innutritious." He brings home the first frog-spittle he finds in a ditch and studies it in a tumbler of water. The first water-beetle that appears he makes a note of, and the first skunk-cabbage that thrusts its spathe up through the mould is of more interest to him than the latest news from Paris or London. "I go to look for mud-turtles in Heywood's meadow," he says, March 23, 1853. The first water-fowl that came in the spring he stalked like a pot-hunter, crawling through the swamps and woods or over a hill on his stomach to have a good shot at them with his — journal. He is determined Nature shall not get one day the start of him; and yet he is obliged to confess that "no mortal is alert enough to be present at the first dawn of spring;" still he will not give up trying. "Can you be sure," he says, "that you have heard the first frog in the township croak?" A lady offered him the life of Dr. Chalmers to read, but he would not promise. The next day she was heard through a partition shouting to some one who was deaf: "Think of it, — he stood half an hour to-day to hear the frogs croak, and he would n't read the life of Chalmers!" He would go any number of miles to interview a muskrat or a woodchuck, or to keep an "appointment with an oak-tree;" but he records in his journal that he rode a dozen miles one day with his employer, keeping a profound silence almost all the way. "I treated him simply as if he had bronchitis and could not speak, — just as I would a sick man, a crazy man, or an idiot."

Thoreau seems to have been aware of his defect on the human side. He says: "If I am too cold for human friendship, I trust I shall not soon be too cold for natural influences;" and then he goes on with this doubtful statement : "It appears to be a law that you cannot have a deep sympathy with both man and nature. Those qualities which bring you near to the one estrange you from the other." One day he met a skunk in the field, and he describes its peculiar gait exactly when he says: "It runs, even when undisturbed, with a singular teter or undulation, like the walking of a Chinese lady." He ran after the animal to observe it, keeping out of the reach of its formidable weapon, and when it took refuge in the wall he interviewed it at his leisure. If it had been a man or a woman he had met, he would have run the other way. Thus he went through the season, Nature's reporter, taking down the words as they fell from her lips, and distressed if a sentence was missed.

The Yankee thrift and enterprise, that he had so little patience with in his neighbors, he applied to his peculiar ends. He took the day and the season by the foretop. "How many mornings," he says in "Walden," "summer and winter, before yet any neighbor was stirring about his business, have I

been about mine!" He had an eye to the main
chance, to a good investment. He probed the
swamps like a butter-buyer, he sampled the plants
and the trees and lichens like a tea-taster. He
made a burning-glass of a piece of ice; he made
sugar from a pumpkin and from the red maple, and
wine from the sap of the black birch, and boiled
rock-tripe for an hour and tried it as food. If he
missed any virtue or excellence in these things or
in anything in his line, or any suggestion to his
genius, he felt like a man who had missed a good
bargain. Yet he sometimes paused in this peeping
and prying into nature, and cast a regretful look
backward. "Ah, those youthful days," he says
in his journal, under date of March 30, 1853, "are
they never to return? when the walker does not too
enviously observe particulars, but sees, hears, scents,
tastes, and feels only himself, the phenomena that
showed themselves in him, his expanding body, his
intellect and heart! No worm or insect, quadruped
or bird, confined his view, but the unbounded universe was his. A bird has now become a mote in his
eye." Then he proceeds to dig out a woodchuck.

In "Walden" Thoreau pretends to quote the
following passage from the Gulistan, or Rose Garden of Sadi of Shiraz, with an eye to its application
to his own case; but as he evidently found it not
in, but under, Sadi's lines, it has an especial significance, and may fitly close this paper: —

HENRY D. THOREAU

"They asked a wise man saying: 'Of the many celebrated trees which the Most High God has created lofty and umbrageous, they call none azad, or free, excepting the cypress, which bears no fruit; what mystery is there in this?' He replied: 'Each has its appropriate produce and appointed season, during the continuance of which it is fresh and blooming, and during their absence dry and withered: to neither of which states is the cypress exposed, being always flourishing; and of this nature are the azads, or religious independents. Fix not thy heart on that which is transitory; for the Dijlah or Tigris will continue to flow through Bagdad after the race of caliphs is extinct; if thy hand has plenty, be liberal as the date-tree; but if it affords nothing to give away, be an azad, or free man, like the cypress.'"

II

SCIENCE AND LITERATURE

INTERESTED as I am in all branches of natural science, and great as is my debt to these things, yet I suppose my interest in nature is not strictly a scientific one. I seldom, for instance, go into a natural history museum without feeling as if I were attending a funeral. There lie the birds and animals stark and stiff, or else, what is worse, stand up in ghastly mockery of life, and the people pass along and gaze at them through the glass with the same cold and unprofitable curiosity that they gaze upon the face of their dead neighbor in his coffin. The fish in the water, the bird in the tree, the animal in the fields or woods, what a different impression they make upon us!

To the great body of mankind, the view of nature presented through the natural sciences has a good deal of this lifeless funereal character of the specimens in the museum. It is dead dissected nature, a cabinet of curiosities carefully labeled and classified. "Every creature sundered from its natural surroundings," says Goethe, "and brought into strange company, makes an unpleasant impression on us, which disappears only by habit." Why is it that the hunter, the trapper, the traveler, the farmer, or even the schoolboy, can often tell us more of what we want to know about the bird, the flower, the animal, than the professor in all the pride of his nomenclature? Why, but that these give us a glimpse of the live creature as it stands related to other things, to the whole life of nature, and to the human heart, while the latter shows it to us as it stands related to some artificial system of human knowledge.

"The world is too much with us," said Wordsworth, and he intimated that our science and our civilization had put us "out of tune" with nature.

> "Great God! I'd rather be
> A Pagan suckled in a creed outworn;
> So might I, standing on this pleasant lea,
> Have glimpses that would make me less forlorn,
> Have sight of Proteus rising from the sea,
> Or hear old Triton blow his wreathed horn."

To the scientific mind such language is simply nonsense, as are those other lines of the bard of Grasmere, in which he makes his poet —

> "Contented if he might enjoy
> The things which others understand."

Enjoyment is less an end in science than it is in literature. A poem or other work of the imagination that failed to give us the joy of the spirit would be of little value, but from a work of science we expect only the satisfaction which comes with increased stores of exact knowledge.

Yet it may be questioned if the distrust with which science and literature seem to be more and more regarding each other in our day is well founded. That such distrust exists is very evident. Professor Huxley taunts the poets with "sensual caterwauling," and the poets taunt the professor and his ilk with gross materialism.

Science is said to be democratic, its aims and methods in keeping with the great modern movement; while literature is alleged to be aristocratic in its spirit and tendencies. Literature is for the few; science is for the many. Hence their opposition in this respect.

Science is founding schools and colleges from which the study of literature, as such, is to be excluded; and it is becoming clamorous for the positions occupied by the classics in the curriculum of the older institutions. As a reaction against the extreme partiality for classical studies, the study of names instead of things, which has so long been shown in our educational system, this new cry is wholesome and good; but so far as it implies that science is capable of taking the place of the great literatures as an instrument of high culture, it is mischievous and misleading.

About the intrinsic value of science, its value as

a factor in our civilization, there can be but one opinion; but about its value to the scholar, the thinker, the man of letters, there is room for very divergent views. It is certainly true that the great ages of the world have not been ages of exact science; nor have the great literatures, in which so much of the power and vitality of the race have been stored, sprung from minds which held correct views of the physical universe. Indeed, if the growth and maturity of man's moral and intellectual stature were a question of material appliances or conveniences, or of accumulated stores of exact knowledge, the world of to-day ought to be able to show more eminent achievements in all fields of human activity than ever before. But this it cannot do. Shakespeare wrote his plays for people who believed in witches, and probably believed in them himself; Dante's immortal poem could never have been produced in a scientific age. Is it likely that the Hebrew Scriptures would have been any more precious to the race, or their influence any deeper, had they been inspired by correct views of physical science?

It is not my purpose to write a diatribe against the physical sciences. I would as soon think of abusing the dictionary. But as the dictionary can hardly be said to be an end in itself, so I would indicate that the final value of physical science is its capability to foster in us noble ideals, and to lead us to new and larger views of moral and spiritual truths. The extent to which it is able to do this measures its value to the spirit, — measures its value to the educator.

That the great sciences can do this, that they are capable of becoming instruments of pure culture, instruments to refine and spiritualize the whole moral and intellectual nature, is no doubt true; but that they can ever usurp the place of the humanities or general literature in this respect is one of those mistaken notions which seem to be gaining ground so fast in our time.

Can there be any doubt that contact with a great character, a great soul, through literature, immensely surpasses in educational value, in moral and spiritual stimulus, contact with any of the forms or laws of physical nature through science? Is there not something in the study of the great literatures of the world that opens the mind, inspires it with noble sentiments and ideals, cultivates and develops the intuitions, and reaches and stamps the character, to an extent that is hopelessly beyond the reach of science? They add something to the mind that is like leaf-mould to the soil, like the contribution from animal and vegetable life and from the rains and the dews. Until science is mixed with emotion, and appeals to the heart and imagination, it is like dead inorganic matter; and when it becomes so mixed and so transformed, it is literature.

The college of the future will doubtless lay much less stress upon the study of the ancient languages; but the time thus gained will not be devoted to the study of the minutiæ of physical science, as contemplated by Mr. Herbert Spencer, but to the study of man himself, his deeds and his thoughts, as illustrated in history and embodied in the great literatures.

"Microscopes and telescopes, properly considered," says Goethe, "put our human eyes out of their natural, healthy, and profitable point of view." By which remark he probably meant that artificial knowledge obtained by the aid of instruments, and therefore by a kind of violence and inquisition, a kind of dissecting and dislocating process, is less innocent, is less sweet and wholesome, than natural knowledge, the fruits of our natural faculties and perceptions. And the reason is that physical science pursued in and for itself results more and more in barren analysis, becomes more and more separated from human and living currents and forces, — in fact, becomes more and more mechanical, and rests in a mechanical conception of the universe. And the universe, considered as a machine, however scientific it may be, has neither value to the spirit nor charm to the imagination.

The man of to-day is fortunate if he can attain as fresh and lively a conception of things as did Plutarch and Virgil. How alive the ancient ob-

servers made the world! They conceived of everything as living, being, — the primordial atoms,
space, form, the earth, the sky. The stars and
planets they thought of as requiring nutriment, and
as breathing or exhaling. To them, fire did not con-
sume things, but fed or preyed upon them, like
an animal. It was not so much false science, as a
livelier kind of science, which made them regard the
peculiar quality of anything as a spirit. Thus there
was a spirit in snow; when the snow melted, the
spirit escaped. This spirit, says Plutarch, "is nothing but the sharp point and finest scale of the con-
gealed substance, endued with a virtue of cutting
and dividing not only the flesh, but also silver and
brazen vessels." "Therefore this piercing spirit,
like a flame" (how much, in fact, frost is like
flame!), "seizing upon those that travel in the snow,
seems to burn their outsides, and like fire to enter
and penetrate the flesh." There is a spirit of salt,
too, and of heat, and of trees. The sharp, acrimo-
nious quality of the fig-tree bespeaks of a fierce and
strong spirit which it darts out into objects.

To the ancient philosophers, the eye was not
a mere passive instrument, but sent forth a spirit,
or fiery visual rays, that went to coöperate with
the rays from outward objects. Hence the power
of the eye, and its potency in love matters. "The
mutual looks of nature's beauties, or that which
comes from the eye, whether light or a stream of

spirits, melt and dissolve the lovers with a pleasing pain, which they call the bitter-sweet of love." "There is such a communication, such a flame raised by one glance, that those must be altogether unacquainted with love that wonder at the Median naphtha that takes fire at a distance from the flame." "Water from the heavens," says Plutarch, "is light and aerial, and, being mixed with spirit, is the quicker passed and elevated into the plants by reason of its tenuity." Rain-water, he further says, "is bred in the air and wind, and falls pure and sincere." Science could hardly give an explanation as pleasing to the fancy as that. And it is true enough, too. Mixed with spirit, or the gases of the air, and falling pure and sincere, is undoubtedly the main secret of the matter. He said the ancients hesitated to put out a fire because of the relation it had to the sacred and eternal flame. "Nothing," he says, "bears such a resemblance to an animal as fire. It is moved and nourished by itself, and by its brightness, like the soul, discovers and makes everything apparent; but in its quenching it principally shows some power that seems to proceed from our vital principle, for it makes a noise and resists like an animal dying or violently slaughtered."

The feeling, too, with which the old philosophers looked upon the starry heavens is less antagonistic to science than it is welcome and suggestive to the human heart. Says Plutarch in his "Sentiments of Nature Philosophers delighted in:" "To men, the heavenly bodies that are so visible did give the knowledge of the Deity; when they contemplated that they are the causes of so great an harmony, that they regulate day and night, winter and summer, by their rising and setting, and likewise considered these things which by their influence in the earth do receive a being and do likewise fructify. It was manifest to men that the Heaven was the father of those things, and the Earth the mother: that the Heaven was the father is clear, since from the heavens there is the pouring down of waters, which have their spermatic faculty; the Earth the mother because she receives them and brings forth. Likewise men, considering that the stars are running in a perpetual motion, and that the sun and moon give us the power to view and contemplate, they call them all Gods."

The ancients had that kind of knowledge which the heart gathers; we have in superabundance that kind of knowledge which the head gathers. If much of theirs was made up of mere childish delusions, how much of ours is made up of hard, barren, and unprofitable details, — a mere desert of sand where no green thing grows or can grow! How much there is in books that one does not want to know, that it would be a mere weariness and burden to the spirit to know; how much of modern physical science is a mere rattling of dead bones, a mere threshing of empty straw! Probably we shall come round to as lively a conception of things by and by. Darwin has brought us a long way toward it. At any rate, the ignorance of the old writers is often more captivating than our exact but more barren knowledge.

The old books are full of this dew-scented knowledge, — knowledge gathered at first hand in the morning of the world. In our more exact scientific knowledge this pristine quality is generally missing; and hence it is that the results of science are far less available for literature than the results of experience.

Science is probably unfavorable to the growth of literature because it does not throw man back upon himself and concentrate him as the old belief did; it takes him away from himself, away from human relations and emotions, and leads him on and on. We wonder and marvel more, but we fear, dread, love, sympathize less. Unless, indeed, we finally come to see, as we probably shall, that after science has done its best the mystery is as great as ever, and the imagination and the emotions have just as free a field as before.

Science and literature in their aims and methods have but little in common. Demonstrable fact is the province of the one; sentiment is the province of the other. "The more a book brings sentiment into light," says M. Taine, "the more it is a work of literature;" and, we may add, the more it brings the facts and laws of natural things to light, the more it is a work of science. Or, as Emerson says in one of his early essays, "literature affords a platform whence we may command a view of our present life, a purchase by which we may move it." In like manner science affords a platform whence we may view our physical existence, — a purchase by which we may move the material world. The value of the one is in its ideality, that of the other in its exact demonstrations. The knowledge which literature most loves and treasures is knowledge of life; while science is intent upon a knowledge of things, not as they are in their relation to the mind and heart of man, but as they are in and of themselves, in their relations to each other and to the human body. Science is a capital or fund perpetually reinvested; it accumulates, rolls up, is carried forward by every new man. Every man of science has all the science before him to go upon, to set himself up in business with. What an enormous sum Darwin availed himself of and reinvested! Not so in literature; to every poet, to every artist, it is still the first day of creation, so far as the essentials of his task are concerned. Literature is not so much a fund to be reinvested as it is a crop to be ever new-grown. Wherein science furthers the eye, sharpens the ear, lengthens the arm, quickens the foot, or extends man farther into nature in the natural bent and direction of his faculties and powers, a service is undoubtedly rendered to literature. But so far as it engenders a habit of peeping and prying into nature, and blinds us to the festive splendor and meaning of the whole, our verdict must be against it.

It cannot be said that literature has kept pace with civilization, though science has; in fact, it may be said without exaggeration that science *is* civilization, — the application of the powers of nature to the arts of life. The reason why literature has not kept pace is because so much more than mere knowledge, well-demonstrated facts, goes to the making of it, while little else goes to the making of pure science. Indeed, the kingdom of heaven, in literature as in religion, " cometh not with observation." This felicity is within you as much in the one case as in the other. It is the fruit of the spirit, and not of the diligence of the hands.

Because this is so, because modern achievements in letters are not on a par with our material and scientific triumphs, there are those who predict for literature a permanent decay, and think the field it now occupies is to be entirely usurped by science. But this can never be. Literature will have its period of decadence and of partial eclipse; but the chief interest of mankind in nature or in the universe can never be for any length of time a merely scientific interest, — an interest measured by our exact knowledge of these things; though it must undoubtedly be an interest consistent with the scientific view. Think of having one's interest in a flower, a bird, the landscape, the starry skies, dependent upon the stimulus afforded by the text-books, or dependent upon one's knowledge of the structure, habits, functions, relations of these objects!

This other and larger interest in natural objects, to which I refer, is an interest as old as the race itself, and which all men, learned and unlearned alike, feel in some degree, — an interest born of our relations to these things, of our associations with them. It is the human sentiments they awaken and foster in us, the emotion of love or admiration, or awe or fear, they call up; and is in fact the interest of literature as distinguished from that of science. The admiration one feels for a flower, for a person, for a fine view, for a noble deed, the pleasure one takes in a spring morning, in a stroll upon the beach, is the admiration and the pleasure literature feels and art feels; only in them the feeling is freely opened and expanded which in most minds is usually vague and germinal. Science has its own pleasure in these things; but it is not, as a rule, a pleasure in which the mass of mankind can share, because it is not directly related to the human affections and emotions. In fact, the scientific treatment of nature can no more do away with or supersede the literary treatment of it — the view of it as seen through our sympathies and emotions, and touched by the ideal, such as the poet gives us — than the compound of the laboratory can take the place of the organic compounds found in our food, drink, and air.

If Audubon had not felt other than a scientific interest in the birds, — namely, a human interest, an interest born of sentiment, — would he ever have written their biographies as he did?

It is too true that the ornithologists of our day for the most part look upon the birds only as so much legitimate game for expert dissection and classification, and hence have added no new lineaments to Audubon's and Wilson's portraits. Such a man as Darwin was full of what we may call the sentiment of science. Darwin was always pursuing an idea, always tracking a living, active principle. He is full of the ideal interpretation of fact, science fired with faith and enthusiasm, the fascination of the power and mystery of nature. All his works have a human and almost poetic side. They are undoubtedly the best feeders of literature we have yet had from the field of science. His book on the earthworm, or on the formation of vegetable mould, reads like a fable in which some high and beautiful philosophy is clothed. How alive he makes the plants and the trees! — shows all their movements, their sleeping and waking, and almost their very dreams, — does, indeed, disclose and establish a kind of rudimentary soul or intelligence in the tip of the radicle of plants. No poet has ever made the trees so human. Mark, for instance, his discovery of the value of cross-fertilization in the vegetable kingdom, and the means Nature takes to bring it about. Cross-fertilization is just as important in the intellectual kingdom as in the vegetable. The thoughts of the recluse finally become pale and feeble. Without pollen from other minds, how can one have a race of vigorous seedlings of his own? Thus all Darwinian books have to me a literary or poetic substratum. The old fable of metamorphosis and transformation he illustrates afresh in his "Origin of Species," in the "Descent of Man." Darwin's interest in nature is strongly scientific, but our interest in him is largely literary; he is tracking a principle, the principle of organic life, following it through all its windings and turnings and doublings and redoublings upon itself, in the air, in the earth, in the water, in the vegetable, and in all the branches of the animal world; the footsteps of creative energy; not why, but how; and we follow him as we would follow a great explorer, or general, or voyager like Columbus, charmed by his candor, dilated by his mastery. He is said to have lost his taste for poetry, and to have cared little for what is called religion. His sympathies were so large and comprehensive; the mere science in him is so perpetually overarched by that which is not science, but faith, insight, imagination, prophecy, inspiration, — "substance of things hoped for, the evidence of things not seen;" his love of truth so deep and abiding; and his determination to see things, facts, in their relations, and as they issue in principle, so unsleeping, — that both his poetic and religious emotions, as well as his scientific proclivities, found full scope, and his demonstration becomes almost a song. It is easy to see how such a mind as Goethe's would have followed him and supplemented him, not from its wealth of scientific lore, but from its poetic insight into the methods of nature.

Again, it is the fine humanism of such a man as Humboldt that gives his name and his teachings currency. Men who have not this humanism, who do not in any way relate their science to life or to the needs of the spirit, but pile up mere technical, desiccated knowledge, are for the most part a waste or a weariness. Humboldt's humanism makes him a stimulus and a support to all students of nature. The noble character, the poetic soul, shines out in all his works and gives them a value above and beyond their scientific worth, great as that undoubtedly is. To his desire for universal knowledge he added the love of beautiful forms, and his "Cosmos" is an attempt at an artistic creation, a harmonious representation of the universe that should satisfy the æsthetic sense as well as the understanding. It is a graphic description of nature, not a mechanical one.

Men of pure science look askant at it, or at Humboldt, on this account. A sage of Berlin says he failed to reach the utmost height of science because of his want of "physico-mathematical knowledge;" he was not sufficiently content with the mere dead corpse of nature to weigh and measure it. Lucky for him and for the world that there was something that had a stronger attraction for him than the algebraic formulas. Humboldt was not content till he had escaped from the trammels of mechanical science into the larger and more vital air of literature, or the literary treatment of nature. What keeps his "Views of Nature" and his "Scientific Travels" alive is not so much the pure science which they hold as the good literature which they embody. The observations he records upon that wonderful tropical nature, that are the fruit of his own unaided perceptions, betraying only the wiser hunter, trapper, walker, and farmer, how welcome it all is! But the moment he goes behind the beautiful or natural reason and discourses as a geologist, mineralogist, physical geographer, how one's interest flags! It is all of interest and value to specialists in those fields, but it has no human and therefore no literary interest or value. When he tells us that "monkeys are more melancholy in proportion as they have more resemblance to man;" that "their sprightliness diminishes as their intellectual faculties appear to increase," — we read with more attention than when he discourses as a learned naturalist upon the different species of monkeys. It is a real addition to our knowledge of nature to learn that the extreme heat and dryness of the summer, within the equatorial zone in South America, produces effects analogous to those produced by the cold of our northern winters. The trees lose their leaves, the snakes and crocodiles and other reptiles bury themselves in the mud, and many phases of life, both animal and vegetable, are wrapped in a long sleep. This is not strictly scientific knowledge; it is knowledge that lies upon the surface, and that any eye and mind may gather. One feels inclined to skip the elaborate account of the physical features of the lake of Valencia and its surroundings, but the old Mestizo Indian who gave the travelers goat's milk, and who, with his beautiful daughter, lived on a little island in its midst, awakens lively curiosity. He guarded his daughter as a miser guards his treasure. When some hunters by chance passed a night on his island, he suspected some designs upon his girl, and he obliged her to climb up a very lofty acacia-tree, which grew in the plain at some distance from the hut, while he stretched himself at the foot of the tree, and would not permit her to descend till the young men had departed. Thus, throughout the work, when the scientific interest is paramount, the literary and human interest fail, and *vice versa*.

SCIENCE AND LITERATURE

No man of letters was ever more hospitable to science than Goethe; indeed, some of the leading ideas of modern science were distinctly foreshadowed by him; yet they took the form and texture of literature, or of sentiment, rather than of exact science. They were the reachings forth of his spirit; his grasping for the ideal clews to nature, rather than logical steps of his understanding; and his whole interest in physics was a search for a truth above physics, — to get nearer, if possible, to this mystery called nature. "The understanding will not reach her," he said to Eckermann; "man must be capable of elevating himself to the highest reason to come in contact with this divinity, which manifests itself in the primitive phenomena, which dwells behind them, and from which they proceed." Of like purport is his remark that the common observations which science makes upon nature and its procedure, "in whatever terms expressed, are really after all only *symptoms* which, if any real wisdom is to result from our studies, must be traced back to the physiological and pathological principles of which they are the exponents."

Literature, I say, does not keep pace with civilization. That the world is better housed, better clothed, better fed, better transported, better equipped for war, better armed for peace, more skilled in agriculture, in navigation, in engineering, in surgery, has steam, electricity, gunpowder, dynamite, — all of this, it seems, is of little moment to literature. Are men better? Are men greater? Is life sweeter? These are the test questions. Time has been saved, almost annihilated, by steam and electricity, yet where is the leisure? The more time we save, the less we have. The hurry of the machine passes into the man. We can outrun the wind and the storm, but we cannot outrun the demon of Hurry. The farther we go, the harder he spurs us. What we save in time we make up in space; we must cover more surface. What we gain in power and facility is more than added in the length of the task. The needlewoman has her sewing-machine, but she must take ten thousand stitches now where she took only ten before, and it is probably true that the second condition is worse than the first. In the shoe factory, knife factory, shirt factory, and all other factories, men and women work harder, look grimmer, suffer more in mind and body, than under the old conditions of industry. The iron of the machine enters the soul; man becomes a mere tool, a cog or spoke or belt or spindle. More work is done, but in what does it all issue? Certainly not in beauty, in power, in character, in good manners, in finer men and women; but mostly in giving wealth and leisure to people who use them to publish their own unfitness for leisure and wealth.

It may be said that science has added to the

health and longevity of the race; that the progress in surgery, in physiology, in pathology, in therapeutics, has greatly mitigated human suffering and prolonged life. This is unquestionably true; but in this service science is but paying back with one hand what it robbed us of with the other. With its appliances, its machinery, its luxuries, its immunities, and its interference with the law of natural selection, it has made the race more delicate and tender, and, if it did not arm them better against disease also, we should all soon perish. An old physician said that if he bled and physicked now, as in his early practice, his patients would all die. Are we stronger, more hardy, more virile than our ancestors? We are more comfortable and better schooled than our fathers, but who shall say we are wiser or happier? "Knowledge comes, but wisdom lingers," just as it always has and always will. The essential conditions of human life are always the same; the non-essential change with every man and hour.

Literature is more interested in some branches of science than in others; more interested in meteorology than in mineralogy; more interested in the superior sciences, like astronomy and geology, than in the inferior experimental sciences; has a warmer interest in Humboldt the traveler than in Humboldt the mineralogist; in Audubon and Wilson than in the experts and feather-splitters who have finished their task; in Watts, Morse, Franklin, than in the masters of theories and formulas ; and has a greater stake in virtue, heroism, character, beauty, than in all the knowledge in the world. There is no literature without a certain subtle and vital blending of the real and the ideal.

Unless knowledge in some way issues in life, in character, in impulse, in motive, in love, in virtue, in some live human quality or attribute, it does not belong to literature. Man, and man alone, is of perennial interest to man. In nature we glean only the human traits, — only those things that in some way appeal to, or are interpretative of, the meaning or ideal within us. Unless the account of your excursion to field and forest, or to the bowels of the earth, or to the bottom of the sea, has some human interest, and in some measure falls in with the festival of life, literature will none of it.

All persons are interested in the live bird and in the live animal, because they dimly read themselves there, or see their own lives rendered in new characters on another plane. Flowers, trees, rivers, lakes, mountains, rocks, clouds, the rain, the sea, are far more interesting to literature, because they are more or less directly related to our natural lives, and serve as vehicles for the expression of our natural emotions. That which is more directly related to what may be called our artificial life, our need for shelter, clothing, food, transportation — such as the factory, the mill, the forge, the railway, and the whole catalogue of useful arts, — is of less interest, and literature is shyer of it. And it may be observed that the more completely the thing is taken out of nature and artificialized, the less interest we take in it. Thus the sailing vessel is more pleasing to contemplate than the steamer; the old grist-mill, with its dripping water-wheel, than the steam-mill; the open fire than the stove or register. Tools and implements are not so interesting as weapons; nor the trades as the pursuit of hunting, fishing, surveying, exploring. A jackknife is not so interesting as an arrow-head, a rifle as a war-club, a watch as an hour-glass, a threshing-machine as the flying flail. Commerce is less interesting to literature than war, because it is more artificial; nature does not have such full swing in it. The blacksmith interests us more than the gunsmith; we see more of nature at his forge. The farmer is dearer to literature than the merchant; the gardener than the agricultural chemist; the drover, the herder, the fisherman, the lumberman, the miner, are more interesting to her than the man of more elegant and artificial pursuits.

The reason of all this is clear to see. We are embosomed in nature; we are an apple on the bough, a babe at the breast. In nature, in God, we live and move and have our being. Our life depends upon the purity, the closeness, the vitality of the connection. We want and must have nature at first hand; water from the spring, milk from the udder, bread from the wheat, air from the open. Vitiate our supplies, weaken our connection, and we fail. All our instincts, appetites, functions, must be kept whole and normal; in fact, our reliance is wholly upon nature, and this bears fruit in the mind. In art, in literature, in life, we are drawn by that which seems nearest to, and most in accord with, her. Natural or untaught knowledge, — how much closer it touches us than professional knowledge! Keep me close to nature, is the constant demand of literature ; open the windows and let in the air, the sun, let in health and strength ; my blood must have oxygen, my lungs must be momentarily filled with the fresh unhoused element. I cannot breathe the cosmic ether of the abstruse inquirer, nor thrive on the gases of the scientist in his laboratory ; the air of hill and field alone suffices.

The life of the hut is of more interest to litera-ture than the life of the palace, except so far as the same Nature has her way in both. Get rid of the artificial, the complex, and let in the primitive and the simple. Art and poetry never tire of the plow, the scythe, the axe, the hoe, the flail, the oar; but the pride and glory of the agricultural warehouse, — can that be sung? The machine that talks and walks and suffers and loves is still the best. Arti-fice, the more artifice there is thrust between us and

Nature, the more appliances, conductors, fenders, the less freely her virtue passes. The direct rays of the open fire are better even for roasting a potato than conducted heat.

What we owe to science, as tending to foster a disinterested love of truth, as tending to clarify the mental vision or sharpen curiosity, or cultivating the spirit of fearless inquiry, or stimulating the desire to see and know things as they really are, would not be easy to determine. A great deal, no doubt. But the value of the modern spirit, the modern emancipation, as a factor in the production of a great literature, remains to be seen.

Science will no doubt draw off, and has already drawn off, a vast deal of force and thought that has heretofore found an outlet in other pursuits, perhaps in law, criticism, or historical inquiries ; but is it probable that it will nip in the bud any great poets, painters, romancers, musicians, orators ? Certain branches of scientific inquiry drew Goethe strongly, but his aptitude in them was clearly less than in his own chosen field. Alexander Wilson left poetry for ornithology, and he made a wise choice. He became eminent in the one, and he was only mediocre in the other. Sir Charles Lyell also certainly chose wisely in abandoning verse-making for geology. In the latter field he ranks first, and in interpreting "Nature's infinite book of secrecy," as it lies folded in the geological strata, he found ample room for the exercise of all the imagination and the power of interpretation he possessed. His conclusions have sky-room and perspective, and give us a sort of poetic satisfaction.

The true poet and the true scientist are not estranged. They go forth into nature like two friends. Behold them strolling through the summer fields and woods. The younger of the two is much the more active and inquiring; he is ever and anon stepping aside to examine some object more minutely, plucking a flower, treasuring a shell, pursuing a bird, watching a butterfly; now he turns over a stone, peers into the marshes, chips off a fragment of a rock, and everywhere seems intent on some special and particular knowledge of the things about him. The elder man has more an air of leisurely contemplation and enjoyment, — is less curious about special objects and features, and more desirous of putting himself in harmony with the spirit of the whole. But when his younger companion has any fresh and characteristic bit of information to impart to him, how attentively he listens, how sure and discriminating is his appreciation! The interests of the two in the universe are widely different, yet in no true sense are they hostile or mutually destructive.

III

SCIENCE AND THE POETS

IT is interesting to note to what extent the leading literary men of our time have been influenced by science, or have availed themselves of its results. A great many of them not at all, it would seem. Among our own writers, Bryant, Irving, Hawthorne, Longfellow, Whittier, show little or no trace of the influence of science. The later English poets, Arnold, Swinburne, Rossetti, do not appear to have profited by science. There is no science in Rossetti, unless it be a kind of dark, forbidden science, or science in league with sorcery. Rossetti's muse seems to have been drugged with an opiate that worked inversely and made it morbidly wakeful instead of somnolent. The air of his "House of Life" is close, and smells not merely of midnight oil, but of things much more noxious and suspicious.

Byron, Shelley, Keats, Landor, seem to have owed little or nothing directly to science; Coleridge and Wordsworth probably more, though with them the debt was inconsiderable. Wordsworth's great ode shows no trace of scientific knowledge. Yet

Wordsworth was certainly an interested observer of the scientific progress of his age, and was the first to indicate the conditions under which the poet could avail himself of the results of physical science. "The Poet," he says, "writes under one restriction only, namely, that of the necessity of giving immediate pleasure to a human Being possessed of that information which may be expected from him, not as a lawyer, a physician, a mariner, an astronomer, or a natural philosopher, but as a Man." "The knowledge both of the Poet and the Man of Science," he again says, "is pleasure : but the knowledge of the one cleaves to us as a necessary part of our existence, our natural and unalienable inheritance ; the other, as a personal and individual acquisition, slow to come to us, and by no habitual and direct sympathy connecting us with our fellow-beings." In reaching his conclusion, he finally says: "The remotest discoveries of the Chemist, the Botanist, or Mineralogist will be as proper objects of the Poet's art as any upon which it can be employed, if the time should ever come when these things shall be familiar to us, and the relations under which they are contemplated by the followers of these respective sciences shall be manifestly and palpably material to us as enjoying and suffering beings. If the time should ever come when what is now called Science, thus familiarized to men, shall be ready to put on, as it were, a form of flesh and blood, the Poet will lend this divine spirit to aid the transfiguration, and will welcome the Being thus produced as a dear and genuine inmate of the household of man." To clothe science with flesh and blood, to breathe into it the breath of life, is a creative work which only the Poet can do. Several of the younger poets, both in this country and in England, have made essays in this direction, but with indifferent success. It is still science when they have done with it, and not poetry. The transfiguration of which Wordsworth speaks is not perfect. The inorganic has not clearly become the organic. Charles DeKay has some good touches, but still the rock is too near the surface. The poetic covering of vegetable mould is too scanty. More successful, but still rather too literal, are several passages in Mr. Nichols's "Monte Rosa." A passage beginning on page 9,

> "Of what was doing on earth
> Ere man had come to see,"

is good science and pretty good poetry.

> "And that unlettered time slipped on,
>   Saw tropic climes invade the polar rings,
>   The polar cold lay waste the tropic marge;
>   Saw monster beasts emerge in ooze and air,
>   And run their race and stow their bones in clay;
>   Saw the bright gold bedew the elder rocks,
>   And all the gems grow crystal in their caves;

Saw plant wax quick, and stir to moving worm,
And worm move upward, reaching toward the brute;
Saw brute by habit fit himself with brain,
And startle earth with wondrous progeny;
Saw all of these, and still saw no true man,
For man was not, or still so rarely was,
That as a little child his thoughts were weak,
Weak and forgetful and of nothing worth,
And Nature stormed along her changeful ways
Unheeded, undescribed, the while man slept
Infolded in his germ, or with fierce brutes,
Himself but brutal, waged a pigmy war,
Unclad as they, and with them housed in caves,
Nor knew that sea retired or mountain rose."

Whether the science in this and similar passages, with which Mr. Nichols's epic abounds, has met with a change of heart and become pure poetry, may be questioned. There is a more complete absorption of science and the emotional reproduction of it in Whitman, as there is also in Tennyson. "In Memoriam" is full of science winged with passion.

Tennyson owes a larger debt to physical science than any other current English poet; Browning, the largest debt to legerdemain, or the science of jugglery. Occasionally Tennyson puts wings to a fact of science very successfully, as in his "The Two Voices:" —

"To-day I saw the dragon-fly
Come from the wells where he did lie.

"An inner impulse rent the veil
Of his old husk: from head to tail
Came out clear plates of sapphire mail.

"He dried his wings: like gauze they grew:
Thro' crofts and pastures wet with dew
A living flash of light he flew."

Keats's touches are often accurate enough for science, and free and pictorial enough for poetry.

"Here are sweet peas, on tiptoe for a flight;
With wings of gentle flush o'er delicate white,
And taper fingers catching at all things,
To bind them all about with tiny rings."

Or this by a "streamlet's rushy banks:" —

"Where swarms of minnows show their little heads,
Staying their wavy bodies 'gainst the streams,
To taste the luxury of sunny beams
Temper'd with coolness, how they ever wrestle
With their own sweet delight, and ever nestle
Their silver bellies on the pebbly sand!"

Only a naturalist can fully appreciate Keats's owl, — "the downy owl," as the quills and feathers of this bird are literally tipped with down, making it soft to the hand and silent in its flight.

On the other hand, it takes a poet to appreciate fully Linnæus's marriage of the plants, and his naming of the calyx the *thalamus*, or bridal chamber; and the corolla, the tapestry of it.

The two eminent poets of our language whose attitude toward science is the most welcome and receptive are undoubtedly Emerson and Whitman. Of the latter in this connection I have spoken elsewhere. Of Emerson I think it may be said that no other imaginative writer has been so stimulated and aroused by the astounding discoveries of physics. There was something in the boldness of science, in its surprises, its paradoxes, its affinities, its attractions and repulsions, its circles, its compensations, its positive and negative, its each in all, its all in each, its subtle ethics, its perpetuity and conservation of forces, its spores and invisible germs in the air, its electricity, its mysteries, its metamorphoses, its perceptions of the unity, the oneness of nature, — there was something in all these things that was peculiarly impressive to Emerson. They were in the direction of his own thinking ; they were like his own startling affirmations. He was constantly seeking and searching out the same things in the realm of ideas and of morals. In his laboratory you shall witness wonderful combinations, surprising affinities, unexpected relations of opposites, threads and ties unthought of.

Emerson went through the cabinet of the scientist as one goes through a book-stall to find an odd volume to complete a set ; or through a collection of pictures, looking for a companion piece. He took what suited him, what he had use for at home.

He was a provident bee exploring all fields for honey, and he could distill the nectar from the most unlikely sources. Science for its own sake he perhaps cared little for, and on one occasion refers rather disdainfully to "this *post-mortem* science." Astrology, he says, interests us more, "for it tied man to the system. Instead of an isolated beggar, the farthest star felt him, and he felt the star." "The human heart concerns us more than the poring into microscopes, and is larger than can be measured by the pompous figures of the astronomer." But where he could turn science over and read a moral on the other side, then he valued it, — then the bud became a leaf or a flower instead of a thorn.

While in London in 1848 he heard Faraday lecture in the Royal Institute on *dia*, or cross magnetism, and Emerson instantly caught at the idea as applicable in metaphysics. "Diamagnetism," he says, "is a law of the *mind* to the full extent of Faraday's idea; namely, that every mind has a new compass, a new north, a new direction of its own, differencing genius and aim from every other mind." In chemistry, in botany, in physiology, in geology, in mechanics, he found keys to unlock his enigmas. No matter from what source the hint came, he was quick to take it. The stress and urge of expression with him was very great, and he would fuse and recast the most stubborn material. There is hardly a fundamental principle of science that he has not turned to ideal uses. "The law of nature is alternation for evermore. Each electrical state superinduces the opposite." "The systole and diastole of the heart are not without their analogy in the ebb and flow of love," and so on. In "Spiritual Laws" he gives a happy turn to the law of gravitation: —

"Let us draw a lesson from nature, which always works by short ways. When the fruit is ripe, it falls. When the fruit is dispatched, the leaf falls. The circuit of the waters is mere falling. The walking of man and all animals is a falling forward. All our manual labor and works of strength, as prying, splitting, digging, rowing, and so forth, are done by dint of continual falling, and the globe, earth, moon, comet, sun, star, fall for ever and ever."

He is an evolutionist, not upon actual proof like Darwin, but upon poetic insight. "Man," he says, "carries the world in his head, the whole astronomy and chemistry suspended in a thought. Because the history of Nature is charactered in his brain, therefore is he the prophet and discoverer of her secrets. Every known fact in natural science was divined by the presentiment of somebody before it was actually verified." Thus that stupendous result of modern experimental science, that heat is only a mode of motion, was long before (in 1844) a fact in Emerson's idealism. "A little heat, that is a little motion, is all that differences the bald, dazzling white and deadly cold poles of the earth from the prolific tropical climates. All changes pass without violence, by reason of the two cardinal conditions of boundless space and boundless time. Geology has initiated us into the secularity of nature, and taught us to disuse our dame-school measure and exchange our Mosaic and Ptolemaic schemes for her large style. We knew nothing rightly for want of perspective. Now we learn what patient periods must round themselves before the rock is formed ; then before the rock is broken, and the first lichen race has disintegrated the thinnest external plate into soil, and opened the door for the remote Flora, Fauna, Ceres, and Pomona to come in. How far off yet is the trilobite! how far the quadruped! how inconceivably remote is man! All duly arrive, and then race after race of men. It is a long way from granite to the oyster; farther yet to Plato and the preaching of the immortality of the soul. Yet all must come as surely as the first atom has two sides."

Indeed, most of Emerson's writings, including his poems, seem curiously to imply science, as if he had all these bold deductions and discoveries under his feet, and was determined to match them in the ideal. He has taken courage from her revelations. He would show another side to nature equally wonderful. Such men as Tyndall confess their obligation to him. His optics, his electricity, his spectrum analysis, his chemical affinity, his perpetual forces, his dynamics, his litmus tests, his germs in the air, are more wonderful than theirs. How much he makes of circles, of polarity, of attraction and repulsion, of natural selection, of

> "The famous might that lurks
> In reaction and recoil,
> Makes flame to freeze, and ice to boil."

He is the astronomer and philosopher of the moral sentiment. He is full of the surprises and paradoxes, the subtle relations and affinities, the great in the little, the far in the near, the sublime in the mean, that science has disclosed in the world about us. He would find a more powerful fulminant than has yet been discovered. He likes to see two harmless elements come together with a concussion that will shake the roof. It is not so much for material that Emerson is indebted to science as for courage, example, inspiration.

When he used scientific material, he fertilized it with his own spirit. This the true poet will always do when he goes to this field. Hard pan will not grow corn; meteroic dust will not nourish melons. The poets add something to the hard facts of science that is like vegetable mould to the soil, like the contributions of animal and vegetable life, and of the rains, the dews, the snows.

Carlyle's debt to science is much less obvious than

that of Emerson. He was not the intellectual miser, the gleaner and hoarder of ideas for their own sake, that Emerson was, but the prophet and spokesman of personal qualities, the creator and celebrator of heroes. So far as science ignored or belittled man or the ethical quality in man, and rested with a mere mechanical conception of the universe, he was its enemy. Individuality alone interested him. Not the descent of the species, but the ascent of personal attributes, was the problem that attracted him. He was unfriendly to the doctrine of physical evolution, yet his conception of natural selection and the survival of the fittest as applied to history is as radical as Darwin's. He had studied astronomy to some purpose. The fragment left among his papers called "Spiritual Optics," and published by Froude in his life of him, shows what a profound interpretation and application he had given to the cardinal astronomical facts. His sense of the reign of law, his commanding perception of the justice and rectitude inherent in things, of the reality of the ideal, of the subordination of the lesser to the greater, of the tyranny of mass and power, have evidently all been deepened and intensified by his absorption of the main principles of this department of physical science. What disturbed him especially was any appearance of chaos, anarchy, insubordination; he wanted to see men governed and duly obedient to the stronger force, as if the orbs of heaven were his standard. He seemed always to see man and human life in their sidereal relations, against a background of immensity, depth beyond depth, terror beyond terror, splendor above splendor, surrounding them. Indeed, without the light thrown upon the universe by the revelations of astronomy, Carlyle would probably never have broken from the Calvinistic creed of his fathers. By a kind of sure instinct he spurned all that phase of science which results in such an interpretation of the universe as is embodied in the works of Spencer, — works which, whatever their value, are so utterly barren to the literary and artistic mind.

The inquisitions of science, the vivisections, the violent, tortuous, disrupting processes, are not always profitable. Wherein nature answers the most easily, cheerfully, directly, we find our deepest interest ; where science just anticipates the natural sense, as it were, or shows itself a little quicker-witted than our slow faculties, as in the discovery of the circulation of the blood, for instance. The real wonder is that mankind should not always have known and believed in the circulation of the blood, because circulation is the law of nature. Everything circulates, or finally comes back to its starting-point. Stagnation is death. The sphericity of the earth, too, — how could we ever believe anything else ? Does not the whole system of things centre into balls, — every form in nature strive to be spherical ?

SCIENCE AND THE POETS

The sphere is the infinity of form, that in which all specific form is merged and lost, or into which it escapes or gets transformed. The doctrine of the correlation and conservation of forces is pointed to by the laws of the mind. The poets have always said it, and all men have felt it; why await scientific proof? The spectroscope has revealed the universality of chemistry, that the farthermost star, as compared with our earth, is bone of her bone and flesh of her flesh. This is a poetic truth as well as a scientific, and is valuable to all men, because the germ of it always lay in their minds. It is a comfort to know for a certainty that these elements are cosmic; that matter is the same, and spirit, or law, the same everywhere; and that, if we were to visit the remotest worlds, we should not find the men rooted to the ground and the trees walking about, but life on the same terms as here. The main facts of natural history also lie in the main direction of our natural faculties, and are proper and welcome to all men. So much of botany, so much of biology, so much of geology, of chemistry, of natural philosophy, as lies within the sphere of legitimate observation, or within the plane of man's natural knowledge, is capable of being absorbed by literature, and heightened to new significance.

IV

MATTHEW ARNOLD'S CRITICISM

WHEN Matthew Arnold, during his visit to this country in 1883–84, delivered himself upon Emerson and Carlyle, he criticised two men who belong to quite a different order of mind from his own, — men who are the prophets of the intuitions and the moral sense, as he himself is the apostle of culture and clear intelligence. Emerson and Carlyle were essentially religious, and were filled with the sentiment of the infinite, which M. Renan regards as the chief gift of mediævalism to the modern world; while Arnold is essentially critical, and is filled with the sentiment or idea of culture, which is the chief gift to the world of Greek civilization. What he had to say of these two men I shall consider in another chapter. At present I wish to take a general view of Arnold's criticism as a whole.

Probably the need for the urbanity and clear reason which Arnold brings is just as urgent as the need for the moral fervor and conviction which Carlyle brings; if not to us in this country, where the conscience of man needs stimulating more than his intellect needs clearing, then certainly in England, where the popular mind is less quick and flexible than in America. And it is against England, against British civilization, that the force of Arnold's criticism has been directed.

The application to America of the main drift of his criticism of British civilization is lessened not only for the reason above hinted at, — namely, that the race refines and comes into shape in this country faster than in Britain, faster, perhaps, than the due proportion between character and faculty will warrant, — but because class distinctions are practically abolished here, and because, in general, there is not the same cramped, inflexible, artificial, and congested state of things in the United States as causes all the woe of England. The defects in our civilization which Arnold pointed out in a paper printed just before he died, — namely, that our country, or our doings in it, are not interesting, that our people are wanting in the discipline of awe and reverence, that we are given to self-glorification, that our newspapers are flippant and sensational, etc. — are self-evident to all candid observers. " In what concerns the solving of the political and social problem, they [the people of the United States] see clear and think straight ; in what concerns the higher civilization, they live in a fool's paradise." It seems to me that the last part of this sentence is just as true as the first part. From the point of view of a good dinner, — a point of view not to be despised by any means, — our country and our achievements in it are very interesting; but from a high and disinterested point of view, — the point of view of art and literature, of the best that is known and thought in the world, — it is not interesting.

It could hardly be otherwise. America is the product of the commercial and industrial age, the age of prose. Nearly all its features are the outcome of a spirit that makes little account of taste or of the beautiful, — the spirit of gain. The spirit that still rules it, and rules more or less all modern European nations, is the spirit of gain, the greed of wealth, and nothing but the ugly, the prosaic, can be born of this spirit. The Old World is the product of quite a different spirit, the religious spirit and the spirit of chivalry and feudalism. Life seems much riper and fuller there, — has much more flavor, and one can well see how a cultivated European would find America almost intolerable.

Yet the two principles of which Arnold makes so much, Hellenism and Hebraism, the power of ideas and the power of conduct, are doubtless more evenly blended in our people than among those of Great Britain. Indeed, it often appears that, if we need more of either, it is of the latter rather than of the former, a little more of the old Hebrew's reverence and depth and solemnity of character, rather than of the Hellene's flexibility and desire to hear or to tell some new thing.

The equality, also, for which Arnold pleads, we already practically have; and the Irish question, the Church and the State question, and the burning question, May a man marry his deceased wife's sister? we have not. But the question of culture, of taste, of literature, of institutions, of science, of obedience, and of a just mean and measure in life, we have, and shall always have, and may the time be far removed when a man who cherishes such lofty ideals upon all these subjects as did Matthew Arnold shall not find eager and improving listeners among us. Arnold meant authority as distinctly as Carlyle did, but the authority of the gentler reason, and not of the hero.

In connecting his name with that of Carlyle, let us note here that he stood as much alone in his arraignment of his countrymen as the great Scotchman did, and was as little identified with any party, sect, or movement. He was just as fearless and wholesale in his criticisms, but far more cool and dispassionate. Carlyle can hardly be said to have been a reasonable being; the secret of his influence was not his reason, but his genius and religious fervor: but there is no getting away from Arnold's reasonableness (not always or commonly a "sweet reasonableness;" there is often a bitter or acrid flavor to it), the clearness and fullness of his demonstration. Hence he was probably more of a thorn in the side of John Bull than was Carlyle; his criticism is harder to answer, and he applied it with an air of teasing deference and simplicity, or of restrained scorn and contempt, which makes it far more irritating than the Scotchman's explosions of wrath and picturesque indignation. Carlyle is much the greater force, much the more impressive and stimulating, but he is also much the more bewildering and misleading. Arnold has reduced the Scotchman's strange mixture of wrath and tenderness, poetry and eloquence, prophecy and philosophy, to a system, and has drawn out of it the pure metal available for a sharp and telling criticism. "Culture and Anarchy," "Friendship's Garland," the "Mixed Essays," the "Irish Essays," are but the "Latter-day Pamphlets" and "Past and Present" running pure and clear. What was like a mountain of mixed ores in Carlyle becomes weapons of polished steel in Arnold. Take this passage from "Past and Present:" —

"Ask Bull his spoken opinion of any matter, — oftentimes the force of dullness can no farther go. You stand silent, incredulous, as over a platitude that borders on the Infinite. The man's Churchisms, Dissenterisms, Puseyisms, Benthamisms, College Philosophies, Fashionable Literatures, are unexampled in this world. Fate's prophecy is fulfilled; you call the man an ox or an ass. But get him once to work, — respectable man! His spoken sense is next to nothing, nine tenths of it palpable *non*-sense; but his unspoken sense, his inner silent feeling of what is true, what does agree with fact, what is doable and what is not doable, — this seeks its fellow in the world. A terrible worker; irresistible against marshes, mountains, impediments, disorder, incivilization; everywhere vanquishing disorder, leaving it behind him as method and order. He 'retires to his bed three days,' and considers!"

In this passage of strong Carlylese, and in many more like it, lies the germ of Arnold's indictment of his countrymen, that they lack intelligence, or *Geist*, ability to deal with ideas, and that they are great only in deeds, in works, or are Hebraic rather than Hellenic.

Carlyle himself was terribly given to Hebraizing, to praising work, energy, force, and to spurning ideas, except when embodied in a man or hero. With him the man of theory, or of ideas, cuts a sorry figure beside the man of practice or of deeds.

"How one loves to see the burly figure of him, — this thick-skinned, seemingly opaque, perhaps sulky, almost stupid Man of Practice, pitted against some light, adroit Man of Theory, all equipped with clear logic, and able everywhere to give you Why for Wherefore. The adroit Man of Theory, so light of movement, clear of utterance, with his bow full-bent, and his quiver full of arrow arguments, — surely he will strike down the game, transfix everywhere the heart of the matter, triumph everywhere, as he proves that he shall and must do? To your astonishment it turns out oftenest No. The cloudy-browed, thick-soled, opaque Practicality, with no logic utterance, in silence mainly, with here and there a low grunt or growl, has in him what transcends all logic utterance ; a Congruity with the Unuttered, the Speakable, which lies atop, as a superficial film, or outer skin, is his or is not his; but the Doable, which reaches down to the world's centre, you find him there."

Here is the voice of Hebraism, strong and triumphant, as in Arnold we have the voice of Hellenism, clear and triumphant. Yet Carlyle was not so much on the side of the man of deeds as opposed to the man of ideas, as he was on the side of reality as opposed to shams. His mistake probably was too great haste in pronouncing all theories shams, and all force beneficent.

The keynote of Arnold's criticism of his countrymen might also be found in Emerson's "English Traits." Emerson charges the English with the same want of ideas, and credits them with the same noble Hebraizing tendency. The English do not look abroad into universality, he said, quoting Bacon. Bacon, he said, marked the influx of idealism into England. "He had imagination, the leisure of the spirit, and basked in an element of contemplation." "German science comprehends the English." The latter is "void of imagination and *free play of thought*," using the very phrase which Arnold has made so telling and significant. Arnold shows his genius in the way he seizes upon and expands these ideas. What was a casual thought or remark with others, in his hands becomes the axis of a great critical system. What was wit, or poetry, or a happy characterization with Carlyle and Emerson, furnishes him the start for a most searching and original analysis.

Arnold was preëminently a critical force, a force of clear reason and of steady discernment. He is not an author whom we read for the man's sake, or for the flavor of his personality, — for this is not always agreeable, — but for his unfailing intelligence and critical acumen; and because, to borrow a sentence of Goethe, he helps us to "attain certainty and security in the appreciation of things exactly as they are." Everywhere in his books we are brought under the influence of a mind which indeed does not fill and dilate us, but which clears our vision, which sets going a process of crystallization in our thoughts, and brings our knowledge, on a certain range of subjects, to a higher state of clearness and purity.

Let us admit that he is not a man to build upon; he is in no sense a founder; he lacks the broad, paternal, sympathetic human element that the first order of men possess. He lays the emphasis upon the more select, high-bred qualities. All his sympathies are with the influences which make for correctness, for discipline, for taste, for perfection, rather than those that favor power, freedom, originality, individuality, and the more heroic and primary qualities.

It is to be owned that there is a quality, a stimulus, and helpfulness, which we must not expect of Arnold; a power of poetry which his poems, perfect as they are, do not afford us, but which we get in much greater measure from poets far his inferior in intelligence and thoroughness of culture, as in a few poems of Keats; a power of prose which his lucid sentences do not hold ; and a power of criticism which his coolness and disinterestedness do not attain to. But this last we must probably go outside of English literature to find.

Arnold was a civilizing and centralizing force. Out of the spirit which he begets, and which begat him, do not come the great leaders and reformers, the one-sided, headstrong, fanatical men, men that serve as the plowshare of the destinies to break up the stubborn glebe of the world; but the wise, the correct, the urbane, the flexible men, the men who reap and enjoy and beautify the world. He says, in effect, there are enough insisting upon force, upon genius, upon independence, upon rights; he will lay the stress upon culture, and upon duties, and upon those things that make for perfection.

The more vital and active forces of English literature of our century have been mainly forces of expansion and revolution, or Protestant forces; our most puissant voices have been voices of dissent, and have been a stimulus to individuality, separatism, and to independence. But here is a voice of another order; a voice closely allied to the best spirit of Catholicism; one from which we shall not learn hero-worship, or Puritanism, or nonconformity, nor catch the spark of enthusiasm, or of evolution, but from which we learn the beauty of urbanity, and the value of clear and fresh ideas.

One never doubts Arnold's ability to estimate a purely literary and artistic force, but one sees that it is by no means certain that he will fully appreciate a force of character, a force of patriotism, of conscience, of religion, or any of the more violent revolutionary forces, — that is, apart from a literary representation of them, — because his point of view does not command these things so completely as it does the other. Emerson was a literary force, but above and beyond that he was a religious force, a force of genius and of good breeding. The dissenters, the English Puritans, the French Huguenots, embody a force of conscience. Carlyle was a force of Puritanism, blended with a force antagonistic to it, the force of German culture, — two forces that did not work well together and which gave him no rest.

Arnold was a literary force of a very high order, but was he anything else? Will he leave any permanent mark upon the conscience, upon the politics,

Matthew Arnold

upon the thought of his countrymen? His works, as models of urbanity and lucidity, will endure; still they do not contain the leaven which leavens and modifies races and times.

The impression that a fragmentary and desultory reading of Arnold is apt to give one, — namely, that he is one of the scorners, a man of "a high look and a proud heart," — gradually wears away as one grows familiar with the main currents of his teachings. He does not indeed turn out to be a large, hearty, magnetic man, but he proves to be a thoroughly serious and noble one, whose calmness and elevation are of great value. His writings, as now published in a uniform edition, embrace ten volumes, to wit: two volumes of poems; two volumes of literary essays, "Essays in Criticism" and a volume made up of "Celtic Literature" and "On Translating Homer;" a volume of mixed essays, mainly on Irish themes; a volume called "Culture and Anarchy" containing also "Friendship's Garland," mainly essays in political and social criticism; three volumes of religious criticism, namely, "Literature and Dogma," "God and the Bible," and "St. Paul and Protestantism," with "Last Essays;" and one volume of "Discourses in America." Of this body of work the eight volumes of prose are pure criticism, and by criticism, when applied to Arnold, we must mean the scientific passion for pure truth, the passion for seeing the thing exactly as it is carried into all fields. "I wish to decide nothing as of my own authority," he says in one of his earlier essays; "the great art of criticism is to get one's self out of the way and to let humanity decide." He would play the rôle of a disinterested observer. Apropos of his political and social criticisms, he says: —

"I do not profess to be a politician, but simply one of a disinterested class of observers, who, with no organized and embodied set of supporters to please, set themselves to observe honestly and to report faithfully the state and prospects of our civilization."

He urges that criticism in England has been too "directly polemical and controversial;" that it has been made to subserve interests not its own, — the interest of party, of a sect, of a theory, or of some practical and secondary consideration. His own effort has been to restore it to its "pure intellectual sphere," and to keep its high aim constantly before him, "which is to keep man from a self-satisfaction which is retarding and vulgarizing ; to lead him toward perfection by making his mind dwell upon what is excellent in itself, and the absolute beauty and fitness of things."

The spirit in which he approaches Butler's "Analogy" is a fair sample of the spirit in which he approaches most of his themes: —

"Elsewhere I have remarked what advantage

Butler had against the Deists of his own time in the line of argument which he chose. But how does his argument in itself stand the scrutiny of one who has no counter-thesis, such as that of the Deists, to make good against Butler? How does it affect one who has no wish at all to doubt or cavil, like the loose wits of fashionable society who angered Butler, still less any wish to mock, but who comes to the 'Analogy' with an honest desire to receive from it anything which he finds he can use?"

Matthew Arnold was probably the most deeply imbued with the spirit of Greek culture of any English man of letters of our time. It is not that he brings a modern mind to classic themes, as has been so often done by our poets and essayists, but that he brings a classic mind to modern themes, herein differing so widely from such a writer, for instance, as Mr. Addington Symonds, who has written so much and so well upon classic subjects, but in the modern romantic spirit, rather than with the pure simplicity of the antique, — in the spirit whose ruling sense is a sense of the measureless, rather than of measure. "Hellenic virtue," says Dr. Curtius, the German historian of Greece, "consisted in measure," — "a wise observance of right measure in all things."

Arnold divides the forces that move the world into two grand divisions, — Hellenism and Hebraism, the Greek idea and the Jewish idea, the power of intellect and the power of conscience. "The

uppermost idea with Hellenism is to see things as
they really are; the uppermost idea with Hebraism
is conduct and obedience. Nothing can do away
with this ineffaceable difference. The Greek quarrel with the body and its desires is that they hinder right thinking ; the Hebrew quarrel with them
is that they hinder right acting." "An unclouded
clearness of mind, an unimpeded play of thought,"
is the aim of the one ; "strictness of conscience,"
fidelity to principle, is the mainspring of the other.
As, in this classification, Carlyle would stand for
unmitigated Hebraism, so Arnold himself stands for
pure Hellenism ; as the former's Hebraism upon
principle was backed up by the Hebraic type of
mind, its grandeur, its stress of conscience, its opu-
lent imagination, its cry for judgment and justice, so
Arnold's conviction of the superiority of Hellenism
as a remedy for modern ills is backed up by the Hellenic type of mind, its calmness, its lucidity, its sense
of form and measure. Indeed, Arnold is probably
the purest classic writer that English literature, as
yet, has to show; classic not merely in the repose and
purity of his style, but in the unity and simplicity of
his mind. What primarily distinguishes the antique
mind from the modern mind is its more fundamental
singleness and wholeness. It is not marked by the
same specialization and development on particular
lines. Our highly artificial and complex modern
life leads to separatism; to not only a division of

labor, but almost to a division of man himself. With the ancients, religion and politics, literature and science, poetry and prophecy, were one. These things had not yet been set apart from each other and differentiated. When to this we add vital unity and simplicity, the love of beauty, and the sense of measure and proportion, we have the classic mind of Greece, and the secret of the power and charm of those productions which have so long ruled supreme in the world of literature and art. Arnold's mind has this classic unity and wholeness. With him religion, politics, literature, and science are one, and that one is comprehended under the name of culture. Culture means the perfect and equal development of man on all sides.

"Culture," he says, giving vent to his Hellenism, "is of like spirit with poetry, follows one law with poetry:" the dominant idea of poetry is "the idea of beauty and of a human nature perfect in all its sides;" this idea is the Greek idea. "Human life," he says, "in the hands of Hellenism, is invested with a kind of aerial ease, clearness, and radiancy; it is full of what we call sweetness and light." "The best art and poetry of the Greeks," he says, "in which religion and poetry are one, in which the idea of beauty and of human nature perfect on all sides adds to itself a religious and devout energy, and works in the strength of that, is on this account of such surpassing interest and instructiveness for us." But Greece failed because the moral and religious fibre in humanity was not braced and developed also.

"But Greece did not err in having the idea of beauty, harmony, and complete human perfection so present and paramount. It is impossible to have this idea too present and paramount; only, the moral fibre must be braced, too. And we, because we have braced the moral fibre, are not on that account in the right way, if at the same time the idea of beauty, harmony, and complete human perfection is wanting or misapprehended amongst us; and evidently it is wanting or misapprehended at present. And when we rely, as we do, on our religious organizations, which in themselves do not and cannot give us this idea, and think we have done enough if we make them spread and prevail, then I say we fall into our common fault of overvaluing machinery."

From the point of view of Greek culture, and the ideal of Greek life, there is perhaps very little in the achievements of the English race, or in the ideals which it cherishes, that would not be pronounced the work of barbarians. From the Apollinarian standpoint, Christianity itself, with its war upon our natural instincts, is a barbarous religion. But no born Hellene from the age of Pericles could pronounce a severer judgment upon the England of to-day than Arnold has in his famous classification of his countrymen into Barbarians, Philistines, and Populace, — an upper class materialized, a middle class vulgarized, and a lower class brutalized. Arnold had not the Hellenic joyousness, youthfulness, and spontaneity. His is a "sad lucidity of soul," whereas the Greek had a joyous lucidity of soul. "O Solon, Solon!" said the priest of Egypt, "you Greeks are always children." But the Englishman had the Greek passion for symmetry, totality, and the Hellenic abhorrence of the strained, the fantastic, the obscure. His were not merely the classical taste and predilections of a scholar, but of an alert, fearless, and thoroughgoing critic of life; a man who dared lay his hands on the British Constitution itself and declare that "with its compromises, its love of facts, its horror of theory, its studied avoidance of clear thought, it sometimes looks a colossal machine for the manufacture of Philistines." Milton was swayed by the Greek ideals in his poetry, but they took no vital hold of his life; his Puritanism and his temper in his controversial writings are the farthest possible remove from the serenity and equipose of the classic standards. But Arnold, a much less poetic force certainly than Milton, was animated by the spirit of Hellenism on all occasions; it was the shaping and inspiring spirit of his life. It was not a dictum with him, but a force. Yet his books are thoroughly of to-day, thoroughly occupied with current men and measures, and covered with current names and allusions.

Arnold's Hellenism speaks very pointedly all through "Culture and Anarchy," in all those assaults of his upon the "hideousness and rawness" of so much of British civilization, upon the fierceness and narrowness, the Jacobinism of parties, upon "the Dissidence of Dissent, and the Protestantism of the Protestant religion;" in his efforts to divest the mind of all that is harsh, uncouth, impenetrable, exclusive, self-willed, one-sided ; in his efforts to render it more flexible, tolerant, free, lucid, with less faith in individuals and more faith in principles. They speak in him when he calls Luther a Philistine of genius ; when he says of the mass of his countrymen that they have "a defective type of religion, a narrow range of intellect and knowledge, a stunted sense of beauty, a low standard of manner ;" that "Puritanism was a prison which the English people entered and had the key turned upon its spirit there for two hundred years;" when he tells the dissenters that in preferring their religious service to that of the established church they have shown a want of taste and of culture like that of preferring Eliza Cook to Milton. "A public rite with a reading of Milton attached to it is another thing from a public rite with a reading from Eliza Cook."

His ideas of poetry as expressed in the preface to his poems in 1853 are distinctly Greek, and they led him to exclude from the collection his long poem called "Empedocles on Etna," because the poem was deficient in the classic requirements of action. He says: —

"The radical difference between the poetic theory of the Greeks and our own is this: that with them the poetical character of the action in itself, and the conduct of it, was the first consideration; with us, attention is fixed mainly on the value of the separate thoughts and images which occur in the treatment of an action. They regarded the whole; we regard the parts. We have poems which seem to exist merely for the sake of single lines and passages, not for the sake of producing any total impression. We have critics who seem to direct their attention merely to detached expressions, to the language about the action, not to the action itself. I verily think that the majority of them do not in their hearts believe that there is such a thing as a total impression to be derived from a poem at all, or to be demanded from a poet; they think the term a commonplace of metaphysical criticism. They will permit the poet to select any action he pleases, and to suffer that action to go as it will, provided he gratifies them with occasional bursts of fine writing, and with a shower of isolated thoughts and images. That is, they permit him to leave their poetical sense ungratified, provided that he gratifies their rhetorical sense and their curiosity."

Here we undoubtedly have the law as deducible from the Greek poets, and perhaps as deducible from the principles of perfect taste itself. Little wonder Arnold found Emerson's poems so unsatisfactory, — Emerson, the most unclassical of poets, with no proper sense of wholeness at all, no continuity, no power to deal with actions. Emerson has great projectile power, but no constructive power. His aim was mainly to shoot a thought or an image on a line like a meteor athwart the imagination of his reader, to kindle and quicken his feeling for beautiful and sublime truths. Valuable as these things are, it is to be admitted that those poems that are concrete wholes, like the organic products of nature, will always rank the higher with a pure artistic taste.

Whatever be our opinion of the value of his criticism, we must certainly credit Arnold with a steady and sincere effort to see things whole, to grasp the totality of life, all the parts duly subordinated and brought into harmony with one another. His watchword on all occasions is totality, or perfection. He has shown us the shortcomings of Puritanism, of Liberalism, and of all forms of religious dissent, when tried by the spirit of Hellenism. We have been made to see very clearly wherein John Bull is not a Greek, and we can divine the grounds of his irritation by the comparison. It is because the critic could look in the face of his great achievement in the world and blame him for being John Bull. The concession that after all he at times in his history exhibited the grand style, the style of the Homeric poems, was a compliment he did not appreciate.

"English civilization, the humanizing, the bringing into one harmonious and truly human life of the whole body of English society, — that is what interests me. I try to be a disinterested observer of all which really helps and hinders that."

He recognizes four principal needs in the life of every people and community, — the need of conduct, the need of beauty, the need of knowledge, and the need of social life and manners. The English have the sense of the power of conduct, the Italians the sense of the power of beauty, the Germans the sense of the power of knowledge or science, the French the sense of the power of social life and manners. All these things are needed for our complete humanization or civilization ; the ancient Greeks came nearer possessing the whole of them, and of moving on all these lines, than any other people. The ground of his preference for the historic churches, the Roman Catholic and the Anglican, over the dissenting churches is that, while they all have a false philosophy of religion, the former address themselves to more needs of human life than the latter.

"The need for beauty is a real and now rapidly growing need in man: Puritanism cannot satisfy it; Catholicism and the English Church can. The need for intellect and knowledge in him, indeed, neither Puritanism, nor Catholicism, nor the English Church, can at present satisfy. That need has to seek satisfaction nowadays elsewhere, — through the modern spirit, science, literature."

He avers that Protestantism has no intellectual superiority over Catholicism, but only a moral superiority arising from greater seriousness and earnestness. Neither have the Greek wholeness and proportion. The attitude of the one toward the Bible is as unreasoning as the attitude of the other toward the church.

"The mental habit of him who imagines that Balaam's ass spoke, in no respect differs from the mental habit of him who imagines that a Madonna, of wood or stone, winked."

The most that can be claimed for each sect, each church, each party, is that it is free from some special bondage which still confines the mind of some other sect or party. Those, indeed, are free whom the truth makes free; but each sect and church has only a fragment of the truth, a little here and a little there. Both Catholic and Protestant have the germ of religion, and both have a false philosophy of the germ.

"But Catholicism has the germ invested in an immense poetry, the gradual work of time and nature, and of the great impersonal artist, Catholic Christendom."

The unity or identity of literature and religion, as with the Greeks, — this is the animating idea of "Literature and Dogma." In this work Arnold brings his Hellenism to bear upon the popular religion and the dogmatic interpretation of the Bible, upon which the churches rest; and the result is that we get from him a literary interpretation of the Bible, a free and plastic interpretation, as distinguished from the hard, literal, and historical interpretation. He reads the Bible as literature, and not as history or science. He seeks its verification in an appeal to taste, to the simple reason, to the fitness of things. He finds that the Biblical writers used words in a large and free way, in a fluid and literary way, and not at all with the exactness and stringency of science or mathematics; or, as Sir Thomas Browne said of his own works, that many things are to be taken in a "soft and flexible sense."

In other words, the aim of Arnold's religious criticism is to rescue what he calls the natural truth of Christianity from the discredit and downfall which he thinks he sees overtaking its unnatural truth, its reliance upon miracles and the supernatural. The ground, he says, is slipping from under these things; the time spirit is against them; and unless something is done, the very heart and core of Christianity itself, as found in the teachings of Christ, will be lost to the mass of mankind. Upon this phase of Arnold's criticism I have this to remark: it is difficult to see how Christianity, as a people's religion, can be preserved by its natural or verifiable truth alone. This natural truth the world has always had; it bears the same relation to Christianity that the primary and mineral elements bear to a living organism: what is distinctive and valuable in Christianity is the incarnation of these truths in a living system of beliefs and observances which not only take hold of men's minds, but which move their hearts.

We may extract the natural truth of Christianity, a system of morality or of ethics, and to certain minds this is enough; but it is no more Christianity than the extract of lilies or roses is a flower garden. "Religion," Arnold well says, "is morality touched with emotion." It is just this element of emotion which we should lose if we reduced Christianity to its natural truths. Show a man the natural or scientific truth of answer to prayer, that is, that answer to prayer is a purely subjective phenomenon, and his lips are sealed; teach him the natural truth of salvation by Jesus Christ, namely, that self-renunciation, that love, that meekness, that dying for others, is saving, and the emotion evaporates from his religion.

It is, he says, the *natural truth* of Christianity that he is after: but it is not the natural truth that the world wants; it is not this that has saved men and that still saves them, that is, holds them up to the standard of their better selves, and sustains

them in a life of solitude and virtue. It is the legend-
ary or artificial truth of Christianity which does
this, that which the human heart, in its fear, its
faith, its hope, its credulity, or in all combined,
supplies. It is what Arnold calls *extra-belief*, or
Aberglaube, the part he is trying to get rid of, that
makes Christianity a power for good over the mass
of mankind. *Aberglaube*, Goethe said, is the poetry
of life, and it is just this superadded element to
Christianity that to the mass of mankind gives its
charm, its attraction, its truth to their hearts and im-
aginations. It is this that touches the natural truth
of Christianity with emotion and makes it fruitful.
It is true that this *Aberglaube* or superstition is
not science, though it perpetually imagines itself to
be so, but it is nevertheless real to the hearts and
faiths of men. To show them that it is not real, that
it is not science, is to strip the tree of its leaves:
the tree will perish ; the natural truth of Christianity will not save it to the masses. They can do
nothing with the natural truth ; the fairy tale, the
extra-belief, or the superstition, — whatever you
please to call it, — must be added. Arnold himself
says: "That the spirit of man should entertain
hopes and anticipations, beyond what it actually
knows and can verify, is quite natural." Yes, and
beyond what is actually true. "Human life could
not have the scope, and depth, and progress it has
were this otherwise."

The reader's mind does not pass readily from Arnold's disbelief in what is called revealed religion to his advocacy of any church or form of worship; from his scientific passion, his effort to see things exactly as they are, to his defense of empty and unmeaning forms. There is a break here, a fault in his mind. There is no logical connection between his attitude in reference to the interpretation of the Bible and his advocacy of a form of religious worship upheld by the state.

If we give up the dogma, we must give up the rite founded upon the dogma. Our churches must become halls of science or temples of art. Can we worship an impersonal law or tendency? If public worship is to be continued, if church organization is still to go on, as Arnold advocates, it is impossible to see how the natural truth of Christianity will alone suffice. The truths of the Bible differ from the truths of science just as a picture or a parable differs from an exact statement; not that they are any more true, but that they are true in a way that makes them take a deeper hold upon the spirit. Science knows as clearly as religion that "the face of the Lord is against them that do evil," but does it know it in just the intimate and personal way? It knows it only as it knows the truth of one of Kepler's laws, by a process of cool ratiocination; but religion knows it through an emotional process, into which the personal elements of love and fear enter.

I am not discussing the superiority of one mode of belief over the other; I only urge that worship has its rise in the latter and not in the former. Reason is not the basis of a national religion, and never has been. It is very doubtful if the disclosure of a scientific basis for the truths of religion would not be a positive drawback to the religious efficacy of those truths, because this view of them would come in time to supplant and to kill the personal emotional view which worship requires.

It is therefore considered as religion, as the basis of public worship, that Arnold does injustice to the popular faith. As science, or philosophy, what he has to offer may be much more acceptable to certain advanced minds, but to the race as a whole a sublimated extract of Christianity can never take the place of the old palpable concrete forms. In fact, getting at the natural truths of a people's religion is very much like burning their temples and their idols and offering them the ashes.

Another form which Arnold's Hellenism takes is that it begets in him what we may call the spirit of institutionalism, as opposed to the spirit of individualism. Greek culture centres in institutions, and the high character of their literary and artistic productions was the expression of qualities which did not merely belong to individuals here and there, but were current in the nation as a whole. With the

Greek the state was supreme. He lived and died
for the state. He had no private, separate life and
occupation, as has the modern man. The arts, architecture, sculpture, existed mainly for public uses.
There was probably no domestic life, no country
life, no individual enterprises, as we know them.
The individual was subordinated. Their greatest
men were banished or poisoned from a sort of jealousy of the state. The state could not endure such
rivals. Their games, their pastimes, were national
institutions. Public sentiment on all matters was
clear and strong. There was a common standard,
an unwritten law of taste, to which poets, artists,
orators, appealed. Not till Athens began to decay
did great men appear, who, like Socrates, had no
influence in the state. This spirit of institutionalism is strong in Matthew Arnold; and it is not
merely an idea which he has picked up from the
Greek, but is the inevitable outcropping of his
inborn Hellenism. This alone places him in opposition to his countrymen, who are suspicious of the
state and of state action, and who give full swing to
the spirit of individualism. It even places him in
hostility to Protestantism, or to the spirit which begat it, to say nothing of the dissenting churches. It
makes him indifferent to the element of personalism,
the flavor of character, the quality of unique individual genius, wherever found in art, literature, or
religion. It is one secret of his preference of the

established over the dissenting churches. The dissenter stands for personal religion, religion as a private and individual experience: the established churches stand for institutional religion, or religion as a public and organized system of worship; and when the issue is between the two, Arnold will always be found on the side of institutionalism. He always takes up for the state against the individual, for public and established forms against private and personal dissent and caprice. " It was by no means in accordance with the nature of the Hellenes," says Dr. Curtius, " mentally to separate and view in the light of contrast such institutions as the state and religion, which in reality everywhere most intimately pervaded one another."

What Arnold found to approve in this country was our institutions, our success in solving the social and political problems, and what he found to criticise was our excessive individualism, our self-glorification, the bad manners of our newspapers, and, in general, the crude state of our civilization.

One would expect Arnold to prefer the religion of the Old Testament to that of the New, for, as he himself says: " The leaning, there, is to make religion social rather than personal, an affair of outward duties rather than of inward dispositions;" and, to a disinterested observer, this is very much like what the religion of the Anglican Church appears to be.

Arnold always distrusts the individual; he sees in him mainly a bundle of whims and caprices. The individual is one-sided, fantastical, headstrong, narrow. He distrusts all individual enterprises in the way of schools, colleges, churches, charities; and, like his teacher, Aristotle, pleads for state action in all these matters. "Culture," he says (and by culture he means Hellenism), "will not let us rivet our attention upon any one man and his doings;" it directs our attention rather to the "natural current there is in human affairs;" and assigns "to systems and to system-makers a smaller share in the bent of human destiny than their friends like."

"I remember, when I was under the influence of a mind to which I feel the greatest obligations, the mind of a man who was the very incarnation of sanity and clear sense, a man the most considerable, it seems to me, whom America has yet produced, — Benjamin Franklin, — I remember the relief with which, after long feeling the sway of Franklin's imperturbable common-sense, I came upon a project of his for a new version of the Book of Job, to replace the old version, the style of which, says Franklin, has become obsolete, and hence less agreeable. 'I give,' he continues, 'a few verses, which may serve as a sample of the kind of version I would recommend.' [1] We all recollect the famous verse in our

---

[1] It turns out that this was only a joke of Franklin's, and it is very curious that Arnold did not see it.

translation: 'Then Satan answered the Lord, and said, Doth Job fear God for nought?' Franklin makes this: 'Does your Majesty imagine that Job's good conduct is the effect of mere personal attachment and affection?' I well remember how, when first I read that, I drew a deep breath of relief, and said to myself: 'After all, there is a stretch of humanity beyond Franklin's victorious good sense!' So, after hearing Bentham cried loudly up as the renovator of modern society, and Bentham's mind and ideas proposed as the rulers of our future, I open the 'Deontology.' There I read: 'While Xenophon was writing his history and Euclid teaching geometry, Socrates and Plato were talking nonsense under pretense of talking wisdom and morality. This morality of theirs consisted in words; this wisdom of theirs was the denial of matters known to every man's experience.' From the moment of reading that, I am delivered from the bondage of Bentham! the fanaticism of his adherents can touch me no longer. I feel the inadequacy of his mind and ideas for supplying the rule of human society, for perfection."

The modern movement seems to me peculiarly a movement of individualism, a movement favoring the greater freedom and growth of the individual, as opposed to outward authority and its lodgment in institutions. It is this movement which has given a distinctive character to the literature of our cen-

tury, a movement in letters which Goethe did more
to forward than any other man, — Goethe, who said
that in art and poetry personal genius is everything,
and that "in the great work the great person is
always present as the great factor." Arnold seems
not to share this feeling; he does not belong to this
movement. His books give currency to another
order of ideas. He subordinates the individual, and
lays the emphasis on culture and the claims of the
higher standards. He says the individual has no
natural rights, but only duties. We never find him
insisting upon originality, self-reliance, character,
independence, but, quite the contrary, on conform-
ity and obedience. He says that at the bottom of
the trouble of all the English people lies the notion
of its being the prime right and happiness for each
of us to affirm himself and to be doing as he likes.
One of his earliest and most effective essays was to
show the value of academies of a central and authoritative standard of taste to a national literature;
and in all his subsequent writings the academic note
has been struck and adhered to. With him right,
reason, and the authority of the state are one. "In
our eyes," he says, "the very framework and exte-
rior order of the state, whoever may administer the
state, is sacred." "Every one of us," he again says,
"has the idea of country, as a sentiment ; hardly
any one of us has the idea of *the state* as a working
power. And why? Because we habitually live in

our ordinary selves, which do not carry us beyond the ideas and wishes of the class to which we happen to belong." Which is but saying because we are wrapped so closely about by our individualism. His remedy for the democratic tendencies of the times, tendencies he does not regret, is an increase of the dignity and authority of the state. The danger of English democracy is, he says, "that it will have far too much its own way, and be left far too much to itself." He adds, with great force and justness, that "nations are not truly great solely because the individuals composing them are numerous, free, and active, but they are great when these numbers, this freedom, and this activity are employed in the service of an ideal higher than that of an ordinary man taken by himself." Or, as Aristotle says, these things must be in "obedience to some intelligent principle, and some right regulation, which has the power of enforcing its decrees."

When the licensed victualers or the commercial travelers propose to make a school for their children, Arnold is unsparing in his ridicule. He says that to bring children up "in a kind of odor of licensed victualism or of bagmanism is not a wise training to give to children." The heads and representatives of the nation should teach them better, but they do nothing of the kind; on the contrary, they extol the energy and self-reliance of the licensed victualers or commercial travelers, and predict full success for their schools. John Bull is suspicious of centralization, bureaucracy, state authority, which carry things with such a high hand on the Continent. Anything that threatens, or seems to threaten, his individual liberty, he stands clear of. The sense of the nation spoke in the words lately uttered through "The Times" by Sir Auberon Herbert. He says: —

"All great state systems stupefy; you cannot make the state a parent without the logical consequence of making the people children. Official regulation and free mental perception of what is right and wise do not and cannot coexist. I see no possible way in which you can reconcile these great state services and the conditions under which men have to make true progress in themselves."

But to preach such notions in England, Arnold would say, is like carrying coals to Newcastle. They would be of more service in France, where state action is excessive. In England the dangers are the other way.

"Our dangers are in exaggerating the blessings of self-will and of self-assertion; in not being ready enough to sink our imperfectly formed self-will in view of a large general result."

There seems to be nothing in Hellenism that suggests Catholicism, and yet evidently it is Arnold's classical feeling for institutions that gives him his marked Catholic bias. The Catholic Church is a great institution, — the greatest and oldest in the world. It makes and always has made short work of the individual. It is cold, stately, impersonal. Says Emerson: —

"In the long time it has blended with everything in heaven above and the earth beneath. It moves through a zodiac of feasts and fasts, names every day of the year, every town and market and headland and monument, and has coupled itself with the almanac, that no court can be held, no field plowed, no horse shod, without some leave from the church."

It appeals to Arnold by reason of these things, and it appeals to him by reason of its great names, its poets, artists, statesmen, preachers, scholars; its imposing ritual, its splendid architecture, its culture. It has been the conserver of letters. For centuries the priests were the only scholars, and its ceremonial is a kind of petrified literature. Arnold clearly speaks for himself, or from his own bias, when he says that "the man of imagination, nay, and the philosopher, too, in spite of her propensity to burn him, will always have a weakness for the Catholic Church;" "it is because of the rich treasures of human life which have been stored within her pale." Indeed, there is a distinct flavor of Catholicism about nearly all of Matthew Arnold's writings. One cannot always put his finger on it: it is in the air, it is in that cool, haughty impersonalism, that *ex cathedra* tone, that contempt for dissenters, that genius for form, that spirit of organization. His mental tone and temper ally him to Cardinal Newman, who seems to have exerted a marked influence upon him, and who is still, he says, a great name to the imagination. Yet he says Newman " has adopted, for the doubts and difficulties which beset men's minds to-day, a solution, which, to speak frankly, is impossible." What, therefore, repels Arnold in Catholicism, and keeps him without its fold, is its " ultramontanism, sacerdotalism, and superstition." Its cast-iron dogmas and its bigotry are too much for his Hellenic spirit; but no more so than are the dogmas and bigotry of the Protestant churches. It is clear enough that he would sooner be a Catholic than a Presbyterian or a Methodist.

The real superiority of the Catholic Church, he says, is in " its charm for the imagination, — its poetry. I persist in thinking that Catholicism has, from this superiority, a great future before it; that it will endure while all the Protestant sects (in which I do not include the Church of England) dissolve and perish. I persist in thinking that the prevailing form for the Christianity of the future will be the form of Catholicism, but a Catholicism purged, opening itself to the light and air, having the consciousness of its own poetry, freed from its sacerdotal despotism, and freed from its pseudoscientific apparatus of superannuated dogma. Its forms will be retained, as symbolizing with the force and charm of poetry a few cardinal facts and ideas simple indeed, but indispensable and inexhaustible, and on which our race could lay hold only by materializing them."

All this may well be questioned. To the disinterested observer, the ritual and the imposing ceremonial of the Catholic Church have about them little of the character of true poetry or of true beauty. These things appeal to a low order of imagination and mentality, and are one secret of the church's influence over the vulgar masses. A man of true taste is no more touched by them than by any rite of pagan faiths. True, the great cathedrals are a part of the ceremonial of the church, and here the height of true poetry is reached, and the imagination is aroused, as it is also by her great names, her poets, artists, scholars, preachers, of the Middle Ages. But the secret of all these things has now passed from the Catholic Church. She is as impotent in art and architecture, in literature and in the pulpit, as are the Protestant churches. Raphaels, and Dantes, and Fénelons, and Pascals, and Bossuets no longer appear within her pale. Should we not rather look for the real superiority of the Catholic Church, as an active force in the world, to its authority, its vast overshadowing power as an institution? In this respect it is nearly perfect, and does indeed touch the imagination. It is as thorough as nature, as searching as fate. It lays its hands upon every force of human life. It is wonderfully adapted to the weakness, the ignorance, and the helplessness of mankind. It establishes the ways, it prescribes your belief, it settles doubts and misgivings. Dr. Johnson said he could easily see how many good but timid and credulous persons "might be glad to be of a church where there are so many helps to get to heaven;" and he adds of himself, "I would be a Papist if I could; I have fear enough, but an obstinate rationality prevents me." It is, indeed, easy to get to heaven by way of the Catholic Church.

It is as complete as Noah's Ark, in which such a motley crew found lodgment. The inmates are housed from the winds, the waves, the storms. Protestantism has taken to the open boats, while some of the sects have hardly a plank beneath them. Yes, if you are no swimmer, and must needs make the voyage with the least possible trouble and exposure, embark in the great mother church. You have little more to do than a passenger on board of one of the Atlantic steamers. Herein we strike the secret of the power of the Catholic Church, and the secret of its hopes for the future. After one has passed through a certain course of experience and development, it is easy to see how men tire of the open boat or single plank mode of navigation, and desire the repose and security of a vessel that has withstood the elements so long. Then people left to themselves do make such wretched work with the

Bible, do belittle and vulgarize it so! They take a text here and a text there, and brood over them, and make a great noise over a nest full of addled eggs; for a text, wrenched from its context and read in any spirit but that in which it was written, becomes as an addled egg. Mormonism is one of the legitimate fruits of Protestantism. The Catholic Church puts an end to all this; there are no more noisy sects and isms; the Bible is authoritatively interpreted. This alone commends her to men of taste.

Arnold's Hellenism is the source of both his weakness and his strength; his strength, because it gives him a principle that cannot be impeached. In all matters of taste and culture the Greek standards are the last and highest court of appeal. In no other race and time has life been so rounded and full, and invested with the same charm. "They were freer than other mortal races," says Professor Curtius, "from all that hinders and oppresses the motions of the mind."

It is the source of his weakness, or ineffectualness, because he has to do with an unclassical age and unclassical people. It is interesting and salutary to have the Greek standards applied to modern politics and religion, and to the modern man, but the application makes little or no impression save on the literary classes. Well might Arnold say, in his speech at the Authors' Club in New York, that only the literary class had understood and sustained him. The other classes have simply been irritated or bewildered by him. His tests do not appeal to them. The standards which the philosopher, or the political economist, or the religious teacher brings, impress them more.

The Greek flexibility of intellect cannot be too much admired, but the Greek flexibility of character and conscience is quite another thing. Of the ancient Hellenes it may with truth be said that they were the "wisest, brightest, meanest of mankind." Such fickleness, treachery, duplicity, were perhaps never before wedded to such æsthetic rectitude and wholeness. They would bribe their very gods. Such a type of character can never take deep hold of the British mind.

When Arnold, reciting the episode of Wragg, tells his countrymen that "by the Ilissus there was no Wragg, poor thing," will his countrymen much concern themselves whether there was or not? When the burden of his indictment of the English Liberals is that they have worked only for political expansion, and have done little or nothing for the need of beauty, the need of social life and manners, and the need of intellect and knowledge, will the English Liberals feel convicted by the charge? When he says of the Pilgrim fathers that Shakespeare and Virgil would have found their company intolerable, is Puritanism discredited in the eye of English Puritans? Indeed, literary standards, applied to politics or religion, are apt to be ineffectual with all except a very limited circle of artistic spirits.

Whether it be a matter for regret or for congratulation, there can be little doubt that man and all his faculties are becoming more and more specialized, more and more differentiated; the quality of unique individual genius is more and more valued, so that we are wandering farther and farther from the unity, the simplicity, and the repose of the antique world.

This fact may afford the best of reasons for the appearance of such a man as Arnold, who opposes so squarely and fairly this tendency, and who draws such fresh courage and strength from the classic standards. But it accounts in a measure for the general expression of distaste with which his teachings have been received. Still, he has shown us very clearly how British civilization looks to Hellenic eyes, where it needs pruning, and where it needs strengthening; and he has doubtless set going currents of ideas that must eventually tell deeply upon the minds of his countrymen.

It is undoubtedly as a critic of literature that Arnold is destined to leave his deepest mark. In this field the classic purity and simplicity of his mind, its extraordinary clearness, steadiness, and vitality, are the qualities most prized. His power as a critic is undoubtedly his power of definition and classification, a gift he has which allies him with the great naturalists and classifiers. Probably no other English critic has thrown into literature so many phrases and definitions that are likely to become a permanent addition to the armory of criticism as has Arnold. Directness and definiteness are as proper and as easy to him as to a Greek architect. He is the least bewildering of writers. With what admirable skill he brings out his point on all occasions! Things fall away from it till it stands out like a tree in a field, which we see all around. His genius for definition and analysis finds full scope in his works on "Celtic Literature," wherein are combined the strictness of scientific analysis with the finest literary charm. The lectures, too, on "Translating Homer," seem as conclusive as a scientific demonstration.

A good sample of his power to pluck out the heart of the secret of a man's influence may be found in his essay on Wordsworth.

"Wordsworth's poetry is great because of the extraordinary power with which Wordsworth feels the joy offered to us in nature, the joy offered to us in simple elementary affections and duties, and because of the extraordinary power with which, in case after case, he shows us this joy and renders it so as to make us share it."

Arnold has been compared to Sainte-Beuve, but

the resemblance is not very striking. Arnold has not the vivacity of mind of the Frenchman, nor the same power to efface himself and his opinions. It is not an easy matter for an Englishman to efface himself on any occasion. Sainte-Beuve is the better instrument, but Arnold is the greater force.

In power of concentration and in power of definition, the English critic surpasses his French master. Sainte-Beuve's power is a power of interpretation; he can adjust himself more closely and happily to a wide diversity of minds than can Arnold. He was not a critic of opinions, doctrines, teachings, but an interpreter of genius in all its forms. No matter what a man taught, so that he taught it well. He has the same pleasure with Pope or Franklin as with Pascal or Massillon. "One loves, one adopts with pleasure," he says, "every kind of genius, every new talent." His mind flows around and around his subject, and envelops it on all sides, and renders the clearest and fullest image of it. He is a pure, disembodied critical spirit, indulging itself to the utmost in the mere pleasure of criticising, of interpreting; taking possession of every form or kind of genius with like ease and enjoyment, blending itself with it, and drawing out its secret by a kind of literary clairvoyance.

Arnold has not, in the same measure, this kind of power. He is less sympathetic and more analytical in his method, and more given to definition and to final judgments. He is also fuller of the spirit of reproof and discipline than the Frenchman. The force of nature and character is less with him, and the authority of the rules and standards more. One would rather submit a bold and original genius to the judgment of the Frenchman; he would see more reason for justifying it upon its own grounds, for allowing it to be a law unto itself; but for a comparative judgment, to know where your original genius departs from the highest standards, wherein he transgresses the law, etc., one would go to Arnold.

A recent English reviewer says that there are but two English authors of the present day whose works are preëminent for quality of style, namely, John Morley and Cardinal Newman. But one would say that the man of all others among recent English writers who had in a preëminent degree the gift of what we call style — that quality in literature which is like the sheen of a bird's plumage — was Matthew Arnold. That Morley has this quality is by no means so certain. Morley is a vigorous, brilliant, versatile writer, but his quality is not distinctively literary, and his sentences do not have a power and a charm by virtue of their very texture and sequence alone. Few writers, of any time or land, have had the unity, transparency, centrality of Arnold's mind, — the piece or discourse is so well cast, it is so homogeneous, it makes such a clear and distinct impression. Morley's vocabulary is the more copious;

more matters are touched upon in any given space; he is more fruitful of ideas and suggestions; his writings may have a greater political, or religious, or scientific value than Arnold's. But in pure literary value they, in my opinion, fall far below. Arnold's work is like cut glass; it is not merely clear, it has a distinction, a prestige, which belongs to it by reason of its delicate individuality of style. The writings of Cardinal Newman have much of the same quality, — the utmost lucidity combined with a fresh, distinct literary flavor. They are pervaded by a sweeter, more winsome spirit than Arnold's; there is none of the scorn, contemptuousness, and superciliousness in them that have given so much offense in Arnold; and while his style is not so crisp as the latter's, it is perhaps more marvelously flexible and magnetic.

Arnold is, above all things, integral and consecutive. He seems to have no isolated thoughts, no fragments, nothing that begins and ends in a mere intellectual concretion; his thoughts are all in the piece, and have reference to his work as a whole; they are entirely subordinated to plan, to structure, to total results. He values them, not as ends, but as means. In other words, we do not come upon those passages in his works that are like isolated pools of deep and beautiful meaning, and which make the value to us of writers like Landor, for instance, but we everywhere strike continuous currents of ideas that set definitely to certain conclusions; always clear and limpid currents, and now and then deep, strong, and beautiful currents. And, after all, water was made to flow and not to stand, and those are the most vital and influential minds whose ideas are *working* ideas, and lay hold of real problems.

Certainly a man's power to put himself in communication with live questions, and to take vital hold of the spiritual and intellectual life of his age, should enter into our estimate of him. We shall ask of a writer who lays claim to high rank, not merely has he great thoughts, but what does he do with his great thoughts? Is he superior to them? Can he use them? Can he bring them to bear? Can he wield them to clear up some obscurity or bridge over some difficulty for us, or does he sit down amid them and admire them? A man who wields a great capital is above him who merely hoards it and keeps it. Let me refer to Landor again in this connection, because, in such a discussion, one wants, as they say in croquet, a ball to play on, and because Landor's works have lately been in my hands, and I have noted in them a certain remoteness and ineffectualness which contrast them well with Arnold's. Landor's sympathies were mainly outside his country and times, and his writings affect me like capital invested in jewels and precious stones, rather than employed in any great and worthy enterprise. One turns over his beautiful sentences with a certain admiration and enjoyment, but his ideas do not fasten upon one, and ferment and grow in his mind, and influence his judgments and feelings. It is not a question of abstraction or of disinterestedness, but of seriousness of purpose. Emerson is more abstract, more given up to ideal and transcendental valuations, than Landor; but Emerson is a power, because he partakes of a great spiritual and intellectual movement of his times; he is unequivocally of to-day and of New England. So with Arnold, he is unequivocally of to-day; he is unequivocally an Englishman, but an Englishman thoroughly imbued with the spirit of Greek art and culture. The surprise in reading Arnold is never the novelty of his thought or expression, or the force with which his ideas are projected, but in the clearness and nearness of the point of view, and the steadiness and consistency with which the point of view is maintained. He is as free from the diseases of subtlety and over-refinement of thought or expression, and from anything exaggerated or fanciful, as any of the antique authors. His distinguishing trait is a kind of finer common-sense. One remembers his acknowledgment of his indebtedness to the sanity and clear sense of Franklin. It is here the two minds meet; the leading trait of each is this same sanity and clear sense, this reliance upon the simple palpable reason.

Arnold's reliance upon the near and obvious reason, and his distrust of metaphysical subtleties and curious refinements, are so constant that he has been accused of parading the commonplace. But the commonplace, when used with uncommon cleverness and aptness, is always the most telling. He thinks the great weakness of Christianity at the present time is its reliance, or pretended reliance, upon the preternatural, and the whole burden of his own effort in this field is to show its basis upon common-sense, upon a universal need and want of mankind. For ingenious, for abstruse reasons Arnold has no taste at all, either in religion, in literature, or in politics, and the mass of readers will sympathize with him. "At the mention of that name *metaphysics*," he says, "lo, essence, existence, substance, finite and infinite, cause and succession, something and nothing, begin to weave their eternal dance before us, with the confused murmur of their combinations filling all the region governed by *her* who, far more indisputably than her late-born rival, political economy, has earned the title of the Dismal Science."

The dangers of such steadiness and literary conservatism as Arnold's are the humdrum and the commonplace ; but he is saved from these by his poetic sensibility. How homogeneous his page is, like air or water! There is little color, little variety, but there is an interior harmony and fitness, that is like good digestion or good health. Vivacity of mind he is not remarkable for, but in singleness and continuity he is extraordinary. His seriousness of purpose seldom permits him to indulge in wit; humor is a more constant quality with him. But never is there wit for wit's sake, nor humor for humor's sake; they are entirely in the service of the main argument. The wit is usually a thrust, as when he says of the Nonconformist that he "has worshiped his fetich of separatism so long that he is likely to wish to remain, like Ephraim, 'a wild ass alone by himself.'" The book in which he uses the weapons of wit and humor the most constantly he calls, with refined sarcasm, "Friendship's Garland," — a garland made up mainly of nettles. Like all of his books, it is aimed at the British Philistine, but it is less Socratic than the other books and contains more of Dean Swift. Arnold is always a master of the artful Socratic method, but this book has, in addition, a playful humor and a nettle-like irony — an itch which ends in a burn — that are more modern. What a garland he drops by the hand of his Prussian friend Arminius upon the brow of Hepworth Dixon in characterizing his style as "Middleclass Macaulayese:" —

"'I call it Macaulayese,' says the pedant, 'because it has the same internal and external characteristics as Macaulay's style; the external characteristic being a hard metallic movement with nothing of the soft play of life, and the internal characteristic being a perpetual semblance of hitting the right nail on the head without the reality. And I call it middle-class Macaulayese because it has these faults without the compensation of great studies, and of conversance with great affairs, by which Macaulay partly redeemed them.'"

By the hand of another character he crowns Mr. Sala thus: —

"But his career and genius have given him somehow the secret of a literary mixture novel and fascinating in the last degree: he blends the airy epicureanism of the *salons* of Augustus with the full-bodied gayety of our English Cider-cellar."

Most of the London newspapers, too, receive their garlands. That of "The Times" is most taking: —

"'Nay,' often this enthusiast continues, getting excited as he goes on, '"The Times" itself, which so stirs some people's indignation, — what is "The Times" but a gigantic Sancho Panza, following by an attraction he cannot resist that poor, mad, scorned, suffering, sublime enthusiast, the modern spirit; following it, indeed, with constant grumbling, expostulation, and opposition, with airs of protection, of compassionate superiority, with an incessant by-play of nods, shrugs, and winks addressed to the spectators; following it, in short, with all the incurable recalcitrancy of a lower nature, but still following it?'"

In "Friendship's Garland" many of the shafts

Arnold has aimed at his countrymen in his previous books are refeathered and repointed and shot with a grace and playful mockery that are immensely diverting. He has perhaps never done anything so artistic and so full of genius. It fulfills its purpose with a grace and a completeness that awaken in one the feeling of the delicious; it is the only one of his books one can call delicious.

Anything like passion, or heat of the blood, Arnold is especially shy of. As Marcus Aurelius said of his imperial father, on all occasions he "stops short of the sweating point." Heat begets fumes and fumes cloud the sky, and Arnold's strength is always in his unclouded intelligence. An unclouded intelligence is among the supreme gifts, but it is not all. Arnold makes us so in love with it that we quite forget the broader and more intensely human qualities, and the part they play in our highest mental operations. Truly, as he says in "Youth and Calm," —

"Calm's not life's crown, though calm is well."

Arnold's desire for calm, for tranquillity, for perfection, probably stands in the way of his full appreciation of certain types of men. All great movements and revolutions are at the expense of calm, of measure, of proportion. A certain bias, a certain heat and onesidedness, are necessary to break the equilibrium and set the currents going.

The master forces of this world, like Luther in religion, or Cromwell in politics, or Victo Hugo or Shakespeare in literature, or Turner in art, are not nicely measured and adjusted. In the modern world, especially, is man onesided, unclassical, fragmentary ; a great talent here, another there, but nowhere the wholeness and totality Arnold pleads for.

V

ARNOLD'S VIEW OF EMERSON AND CARLYLE

DURING Matthew Arnold's first visit to this country, in 1883–84, he lectured in various cities upon Emerson, with whose name he linked that of Carlyle. I had the pleasure of hearing him in New York on the occasion of the second or third repetition of his lecture in that city. Some weeks previously I had met him at a reception at the house of a friend. In my note-book I find I made the following note of the impression he made upon me on this occasion: "Liked him better than I expected to. A large, tall man with black hair streaked with gray, black close-cut side-whiskers, prominent nose, large coarse (but pure) mouth and muscular neck. In fact a much coarser man than you would expect to see, and stronger-looking. A good specimen of the best English stock, plenty of color, a wholesome coarseness and open-air look. One would say that he belonged to a bigger and more powerful race than the rest of the people in the room. His voice was more husky, more like a sailor's, I thought, than the other voices I heard. When he talks to you he throws his head back (the reverse of Emerson's manner), and looks out from under his heavy eyelids, and sights you down his big nose — draws off, as it were, and gives you his chin. It is the critical attitude, not the sympathetic. Yet he does not impress one as cold and haughty, but quite the contrary."

He was not an entertaining speaker; his voice was too thick and foggy. One would rather read his discourse than hear it.

To one who knows Arnold's devotion to the classic standards, the calm and moderation of Greek art, his verdict upon such writers as Emerson and Carlyle will not be much of a surprise. Tried by the classic standards, both these illustrious men are undoubtedly barbarians. Emerson has indeed the lofty serenity of Greek art, but his fragmentary character, his mysticism, his exaggeration, his ceaseless effort to surprise, are anything but classical. The distinctive features of classic literature, its repose, its measure, its subordination of parts, and hence its wholeness, he probably cared little for. Speaking in one of his essays of how Greek sculpture has melted away like ice and snow in the spring, he says: "The Greek letters last a little longer, but are always passing under the same sentence, and tumbling into the inevitable pit which the creation of new thought opens for all that is old." Carlyle is a barbarian in his style, his uncouthness, his vehe-

mence, his despair, his prejudices, and in the open
conflict and incongruity between his inherited and
his acquired traits, — between his German culture,
which was from without, and his Scotch Presbyteri-
anism, which was from within. Carlyle had no tranquillity; the waters of his soul were lashed into fury
the whole time. The Greek was at ease in Zion, as
Mr. Arnold somewhere says, but think of Carlyle
being at ease in Zion! Indeed, one must put his
classic standards behind him when he gives an un-
qualified admiration to either Emerson or Carlyle
as men of letters.

The force of Arnold's criticism came from the fact
that it was by a man who had a real and tangible
point of view of his own, and who, therefore, gave
a real and consistent account of the subject he dis-
cussed. His view of Emerson was not the view of
Emerson generally held in this country, but it was
such a view of him as puts any man who holds a
contrary one upon his mettle, and challenges him to
give as good an account of his own faith. Much of
the writing upon Emerson had been indiscriminat-
ing, and by men who had no definite point of view
of their own. Even Mr. Morley's essay recently
published is not so satisfying a piece of work as
Arnold's, though he arrives at nearly the same conclusions; but he wanders more in reaching them;
his course is not so direct and steady; in fact, the
point of view is not so clear and definite. He may

conduct us to as commanding a height, but there is often a tangle of words and fine phrases in the way.

But it is the great merit of Matthew Arnold as a critic that he always has a clear and unmistakable point of view, that he always knows his point of view and never wanders far from it. The opening passages of Arnold's lecture were in a strain of such noble and impressive eloquence that I must indulge myself in transcribing some of them here.

"Forty years ago," he began, "when I was an undergraduate at Oxford, voices were in the air then which haunt my memory still. Happy the man who in that susceptible season of youth hears such voices! they are a possession to him forever. No such voices as those we heard in our youth at Oxford are sounding there now. Oxford has more criticism now, more knowledge, more light; but such voices as those of our youth it has no longer. The name of Cardinal Newman is a great name to the imagination still; his genius and his style are still things of power. But he is over eighty years old; he is in the Oratory at Birmingham; he has adopted for the doubts and difficulties which beset men's minds to-day a solution which, to speak frankly, is impossible. . . . But there were other voices sounding in our ears besides Newman's. There was the puissant voice of Carlyle, so sorely strained, overused, and misused since, but then fresh, comparatively sound, and reaching our hearts with true pathetic eloquence. . . . A greater voice still — the greatest voice of the century — came to us in those youthful years through Carlyle: the voice of Goethe. . . . And beside those voices there came to us in that old Oxford time a voice also from this side of the Atlantic, — a clear and pure voice, which, for my ear at any rate, brought a strain as new, and moving, and unforgettable as the strain of Newman or Carlyle or Goethe. Mr. Lowell has well described the apparition of Emerson, to your young generation here, in the distant time of which I am speaking, and of his workings upon them. He was your Newman, your man of soul and genius visible to you in the flesh, speaking to your bodily ears, — a present object for your heart and imagination. That is surely the most potent of all influences! nothing can come up to it. To us at Oxford, Emerson was but a voice speaking from three thousand miles away. But so well he spoke that from that time forth Boston Bay and Concord were names invested to my ear with a sentiment akin to that which invests for me the names of Oxford and Weimar ; and snatches of Emerson's strain fixed themselves in my mind as imperishably as any of the eloquent words which I have been just now quoting."

A lofty and eloquent introduction was that, and one well worth the subject and the occasion. The disappointment and irritation which his hearers felt as the lecturer proceeded arose from the fact that the critic was at much less pains to justify this favorable view of Emerson, which he had sounded in his opening note, than he was to establish the adverse view of him as a poet and philosopher which he felt sure would in time be taken. The gist of the speaker's view of Emerson was briefly as follows: Emerson was not a great poet, was not to be ranked among the legitimate poets, because his poetry had not the Miltonic requirements of simplicity, sensuousness, and passion. He was not even a great man of letters, because he had not a genius and instinct for style ; his style had not the requisite wholeness of good tissue. Who were the great men of letters ? They were Plato, Cicero, Voltaire, La Bruyère, Milton, Addison, Swift, — men whose prose is by a kind of native necessity true and sound. Emerson was not a great philosopher, because he had no constructive talent, — he could not build a system of philosophy. What, then, was his merit ? He was to be classed with Marcus Aurelius, who was "the friend and aider of those who would live in the spirit." This was Emerson's chief merit and service: he was the friend and aider of those who would live in the spirit. The secret of his influence was not in his thought; it was in his temper, his unfaltering spirit of cheerfulness and hope.

In the opinion of the speaker, even Carlyle was not a great writer, and his work was of much less importance than Emerson's. As Wordsworth's poetry was the most important work done in verse in our language during the nineteenth century, so Emerson's essays were, in the lecturer's view, the most important work done in prose. Carlyle was not a great writer, because he was too impatient, too willful, too vehement; he did not work his material up into good literary form.

In his essay on Joubert, Arnold says, following a remark of Sainte-Beuve, that as to the estimate of its own authors every nation is the best judge (the positive estimate, not the comparative, as regards the authors of other countries), and that, therefore, a foreigner's judgments about the intrinsic merits of a nation's authors will generally, when at complete variance with that nation's own, be wrong. Arnold's verdict upon Emerson's intrinsic merits was certainly at variance with that of the best judges among Emerson's countrymen, and is likely, therefore, according to the above dictum, to be wrong. But whether it was or not, it is no doubt true that every people possesses a key to its own great men, or to those who share its tendencies and hopes, that a foreigner cannot possess, whatsoever keys of another sort he may bring with him.

From Arnold's point of view, his criticism of Emerson was just and consistent; but he said he spoke not of himself, but assumed to anticipate the verdict of time and fate upon this man. But time and fate have ways of their own in dealing with reputations, and the point of view of the future with reference to this subject is, I imagine, as likely to be different from Mr. Arnold's as it is to be one with it.

In the view which the speaker took of Emerson and Carlyle, it seems to me that he laid too little stress upon their intrinsic quality of genius and of the real force and stimulus they left embodied in literary forms, — imperfect or inadequate forms if you will, but still *literary* forms. Did the speaker draw out for us and impart to us what of worth and significance there was in these men? Did he convey to us a lively impression of their genius? I think not. And yet he has told us in his essay on Joubert that this is the main matter; he asks, "What is really precious and inspiring, in all that we get from literature, except this sense of an immediate contract with genius itself, and the stimulus toward what is true and excellent which we derive from it?" Like all other writers, when Arnold speaks from the traditions of his culture and the influence of his environment, he is far less helpful and satisfactory than when he speaks from his native genius and insight, and gives free play to that wonderfully clear, sensitive, flexible, poetic mind of his. And in this verdict upon Emerson and Carlyle, it seems to me, he speaks more from his bias, more from his dislike of nonconformists, than from his genius.

We have had much needed service from Arnold; he has taught his generation the higher criticism, as

Sainte-Beuve taught it to his. A singularly logical and constructive mind, yet a singularly fluid and interpretative one, giving to his criticism charm, as well as force and penetration.

All of his readers know how free he is from anything strained or fantastic or paradoxical, and how absolutely single is his eye. His page flows as limpid and tranquil as a meadow brook, loitering under this bank and under that, but yet really *flowing*, really abounding in continuous currents of ideas that lead to large and definite results. His works furnish abundant illustrations of the principle of evolution in literature which he demands of others. He makes no use of the Emersonian method of surprise; his ideas never suddenly leap out full-grown from his brain, but slowly develop and unfold before you, and there are no missing links. Any given thought is continuous with him, and grows and expands with new ramifications and radiations, from year to year. This gives a wonderful consecutiveness and wholeness to his work, as well as great clearness and simplicity. Yet one sometimes feels as if his keen sense of form and order sometimes stood between him and the highest truths. I believe the notions we get from him of the scope and function of poetry, and of the value and significance of style, are capable of revision.

Less stringency of form is to be insisted upon, less servility to the classic standards. We live in an age

of expansion, not of concentration, as Arnold long
ago said; "like the traveler in the fable, therefore,
we begin to wear our cloak a little more loosely."
In literature we are coming more and more to look
beyond the form into the substance; yea, into the
mood and temper that begat the substance.

"The chief trait of any given poet," says a recent
authority, "is always the spirit he brings to the
observation of humanity and nature, — the mood
out of which he contemplates his subject. What
kind of temper and what amount of faith reports
these things?"

Of like purport is the well-known passage of
Sainte-Beuve, wherein, after referring to the demands and standards of the classic age, he says that
for us to-day "the greatest poet is not he who has
done the best," — that is, written the most perfect
poem from the classic standpoint; "it is he who suggests the most, — he, not all of whose meaning is at
first obvious, and who leaves you much to desire, to
explain, to study, much to complete in your turn."

In the decay of the old faiths, and in the huge
aggrandizement of physical science, the refuge and
consolation of serious and truly religious minds is
more and more in literature, and in the free escapes
and outlooks which it supplies. The best modern
poetry and the best modern prose take down the
bars for us and admit us to new and large fields of
moral and intellectual conquest in a way the antique

authors could not and did not aim to do. New wants, and therefore new standards, have arisen. Purely literary poets like Shakespeare and Milton, priceless as they are, are of less service to mankind in an age like ours, when religion is shunned by the religious soul, than the more exceptional poets and writers, like Goethe and Carlyle, or Wordsworth and Emerson, — the wise physicians and doctors who also minister to our wants as moral and spiritual beings.

The type of men of which Emerson and Carlyle are the most pronounced and influential examples in our time, it must be owned, is comparatively a new turn-up in literature, — men whose highest distinction is the depth and fervor of their moral conviction, whose greatness of character is on a par with their greatness of intellect; a new style of man writing poems, essays, criticisms, histories, and filling these forms with a spirit and a suggestiveness far more needful and helpful to us in these times than the mere spirit of perfection in letters, — the classic spirit, which Mr. Arnold himself so assiduously cultivates.

To say that Carlyle is not a great writer, or, more than that, a supreme literary artist, is to me like denying that Angelo and Rembrandt were great painters, or that the sea is a great body of water. His life of herculean labor was entirely given to letters, and he undoubtedly brought to his tasks the greatest single equipment of pure literary talent English prose has ever received. Beside some of the men named by the lecturer, his illuminating power is like the electric light beside a tallow dip. Not a perfect writer certainly, nor always an agreeable one; but he exhibited at all times the traits which the world has consented to call great. He bequeathed to mankind an enormous intellectual force and weight of character, embodied in enduring literary forms.

I know it has become the fashion to disparage Carlyle's histories; it is said he has been superseded by the more scientific historians. When the scientific artist supersedes Michael Angelo, and the scientific poet supersedes Shakespeare, then probably the scientific historian will supersede Carlyle. The scientific spirit, when applied to historical problems, is — like chemistry applied to agriculture — valuable, but great results have been achieved in quite another spirit. Scientific method can exhume the past, but cannot breathe the breath of life into it, as Carlyle did. Your scientific critic is usually a wearisome creature. We do not so much want history explained after the manner of science as we want it portrayed and interpreted after the manner of literature. And the explanations of these experts are usually only clever thimble-rigging. If they ferret the mystery out of one hole, they run it to cover in another. How clever, for instance, is Taine's explanation of those brilliant epochs in the history of nations when groups of great men are produced, and literatures and arts get founded! Why, it is only the result of a hidden "concord of creative forces;" and the opposite periods, the periods of sterility, are the result of "inward contrarieties." Truly, a rose by any other name would smell as sweet. What causes the hidden concord, etc., so that we can lay our hand upon the lever and bring about the splendid epochs at a given time, the astute Frenchman does not tell us. I like better the explanation of the old Roman, Paterculus, namely, emulation among men; yes, and emulation in Nature herself. One great orator or poet will make others. Or Emerson's suggestion, which is just as near the truth, and much more taking to the imagination: —

"Heats or genial periods arrive in history, or, shall we say, plenitudes of Divine Presence, by which high tides are caused in the human spirit, and great virtues and talents appear, as in the eleventh, twelfth, thirteenth, and again in the sixteenth and seventeenth centuries, when the nation (England) was full of genius and piety."

Carlyle's bias does not, in my opinion, mar his histories at all, and we can always allow for it when he writes upon any subject, — upon America, for instance, or "Shooting Niagara." It does not mar his "Cromwell," but lends zest to it. He was himself the fiery partisan he was portraying. It does not mar "Frederick," though the author's partialities and prepossessions crop out on every page. What vivid portraiture, what rapid grouping, what *reality*, what exhaustless wit and humor, what entertainment for both heart and head, this book holds!

Most readers of "Frederick," I imagine, find the work too long, and at times feel a strong inclination to "skip," an inclination which the author himself favors by putting his less important matter in finer type. A little more rigid selection and abridgment, and a little more patient fusing of the material so as to have brought the work within the compass of one third less space, and within the compass of the author's best time and strength, and literature would have been the gainer.

Carlyle's prose has its defects most assuredly. His periods are often like those swelled bricks that have got too much of the fire, — crabbed and perverse. His earnestness, his fury of conviction, made it too hot for them; his style becomes distorted. In the best prose there is always a certain smoothness and homogeneity. "In the very torrent, tempest, and (as I may say) whirlwind of your passion," says Hamlet in his address to the players, "you must acquire and beget a temperance that will give it smoothness." If not external smoothness, then certainly internal, — a fusion or blending that is like good digestion. Carlyle does not always have this; Emerson does not always have it; Whitman does not always have it, probably does not always strive for it; Browning rarely or never has it. There is a good deal in Carlyle that is difficult, not in thought but in expression. To the reader it is a kind of mechanical difficulty, like walking over boulders. In his best work, like the life of Sterling, his essays on Johnson and Voltaire, and the battle-pieces in "Frederick," there is the least of this.

"There is a point of perfection in art," says La Bruyère, " as there is of goodness and ripeness in nature. He who feels and loves it has perfect taste; he who feels it not, who loves something beneath or beyond it, has faulty taste." In the life of Sterling, more completely than in any other one of his books, Carlyle attains to this goodness and ripeness of nature. He is calm and mellow; there is nothing to inflame him, but everything to soften and quiet him; and his work is of unrivaled richness in all the noblest literary qualities. But at other times he was after something beneath or beyond the point of perfection in art. He was not primarily a critical or literary force like Arnold himself, but a moral force working in and through literature. He was the conscience of his country and times, wrought up to an almost prophetic fervor and abandonment, and to cut deep was more a point with him than to cut smooth.

Again, his defects as a writer probably arose out of his wonderful merits as a talker. He was in the first instance a talker, and he came finally to write as he talked, so that the page, to retain all its charm and effectiveness, needs the Carlyle voice and manner, and the Carlyle laugh superadded. These would give it smoothness and completion. One rather likes a certain roughness in a man's style, but it must be a smooth roughness; the roughness of a muscular arm, and not of a malformed or an ill-shapen one.

Of course all these considerations tell against Carlyle's claim to be considered a great writer; yet one may freely admit them and still call him a great writer. Style alone does not make the great writer, any more than faultless tactics make the great general; and the upshot of Carlyle's literary life is an array of volumes, not without serious blemishes, it is true, like the campaigns of Frederick or Wellington or Grant, but which, nevertheless, represent a solidity and splendor of achievement such as the world calls great.

Arnold criticised what he called Carlyle's "perverse attitude towards happiness," but it was only a cheap, easy happiness that Carlyle railed against. He taught that there was a higher happiness, namely, blessedness, — the spiritual fruition that comes through renunciation of self, the happiness of heroes that comes from putting thoughts of happiness out of sight; and that the direct and persistent wooing of fortune for her good gifts was selfish and unmanly, — a timely lesson at all seasons.

Emerson, too, is a great figure in modern literary

history, and to his worth and significance, in this connection, the speaker did very inadequate justice. We know there is much in Emerson's works that will not stand rigid literary tests; much that is too fanciful and ethereal, too curious and paradoxical, — not real or *true*, but only seemingly so, or so by a kind of violence and disruption. The weak place in him as a literary artist is probably his want of continuity and the tie of association, — a want which, as he grew old, became a disease, and led to a break in his mind like that of a bridge with one of the piers gone, and his power of communication was nearly or quite lost. Anything like architectural completeness Emerson did not possess. There is no artistic conception that runs the length and breadth of any of his works; no unity of scheme or plan like that of an architect, or of a composer, that makes an inevitable whole of any of his books or essays; seldom a central and leading idea of which the rest are but radiations and unfoldings. His essays are fragmentary, — successions of brilliant and startling affirmations or vaticinations, with little or no logical sequence. In other words, there are seldom any *currents* of ideas in Emerson's essays, but sallies and excursions of the mind, as if to get beyond the region of rational thinking into the region of surmise and prophecy, — jets and projectiles of thought under great pressure, the pressure of the moral genius. He says, speaking more for himself than for others:

"We learn to prefer imperfect theories and sentences, which contain glimpses of the truth, to digested systems which have no one valuable suggestion." It would be almost impossible to condense any of his essays; they are the last results of condensation; we can only cut them up and abridge them. So far as this criticism tells against Emerson as a literary artist, it must be allowed.

Emerson speaks slightingly of logic, but his own prose is undoubtedly the best when it is the most logical, — that is, the most consecutive and flowing. Logic in this sense is no more the enemy of spontaneity than his method of bold guessing is. "Logic," he says, "is the procession or proportionate unfolding of the intuition." This "unfolding" is indispensable to all good prose, and Arnold did not lay too much stress upon it. Emerson's prose does not always have it; and just in proportion as it is without it is it unsound prose. When the reader comes upon a continuous passage in the essays, one in which the thought is unfolded and carried along from point to point, how easily and joyously the mind passes over it! It is like a continuous path, after we have been picking our way from one isolated stone to another. The first chapter in "Representative Men," on the use of great men, is a stony and broken path; the mind labors more or less in getting through it; but the chapters that follow have much more unity and wholeness, —

much more smoothness and continuity of thought. So has "English Traits" more consecutiveness and unity than the essays. Among the essays, those on Books, on Immortality, on Nature, on Beauty, on Self-Reliance, have more logical sequence and evolution than certain others.

Emerson's style is best when he is dealing with something real and tangible before him, as in his biographical and descriptive papers and his "English Traits," and poorest in his "Dial" papers. His letters often seem stilted and affected, but they nevertheless contain many samples of his best prose. Take this from a letter to Carlyle about "Frederick:" "But the manner of it! — the author sitting as Demiurgus, trotting out his manikins, coaxing and bantering them, amused with their good performance, patting them on the back, and rating the naughty dolls when they misbehave; and communicating his mind ever in measure, just as much as the young public can understand; hinting the future, when it would be useful; recalling now and then illustrative anecdotes of the actor, impressing the reader that he is in possession of the entire history centrally seen, that his investigation has been exhaustive, and that he descends, too, on the petty plot of Prussia from higher and cosmical surveys."

Who will say that the pen which wrote that is not capable of good and sound prose as well as of very acute and telling criticism? Carlyle's egotism and patronizing ways in his histories have never been better touched off.

If Emerson did not have the gift of style in the rather exclusive sense in which Arnold uses the term, he had something which is a very good substitute for it, — he had a fresh, tonic quality of mind which he imparted to nearly everything he wrote. A man's use of language reveals the very fibre and texture of his mind. Silk is silk and hemp is hemp, and the hand knows the difference wherever it touches them; but in literature the same words are silk or hemp according to the mind that uses them. Emerson's page nearly always makes the impression of this finer and more precious quality, and, whatever may be its defects, it belongs to literature pure and simple.

Probably the best test of good prose is this: It is always creative ; it begets in the mind of the reader a deep and pervading sense of life and reality. Now that Arnold is gone, how many writers of creative prose are there in England ? Now that Emerson is gone, how many are there in America ? Is Mr. Gladstone's prose creative ? Far from it, I think. Is Mr. Ruskin's ? With all his brilliancy, I think Ruskin lacks the creative touch. Emerson falls short of it many times, but at his best the creative power of the best prose was assuredly his. He often had that felicity of utterance that diffuses such light and joy in the mind.

EMERSON AND CARLYLE

The greatness of his work consists in the measure of pure genius and of inspiration to noble and heroic conduct which it holds. As a writer he had but one aim, namely, to inspire, to wake up his reader or hearer to the noblest and the highest there was in him; and it was no part of his plan to enter into competition with the Addisonian writers for the production of perfect literary work, — perfect from the standpoint of extrinsic form, argument, logic, evolution. His purpose did not require it, his genius did not demand it. He was to scatter the seed-germs of nobler thinking and living, not to rear a temple to the Muses; and from our point of view the former is by far the more important service. To get at the full worth of Emerson, I say, we must appraise him for his new and fundamental quality of genius, not for his mere literary accomplishments, great as these were.

If it is replied that this is just what the lecturer did, I say the word of highest praise, all through the discourse, was given to the master of mere literary form. There was a tone of disparagement toward Emerson as a man of letters, when there should have been generous approval of the quickening and liberating spirit he brought to letters.

Emerson's message is of the highest importance, and he renders it with rare effectiveness and charm. His page is an enticement to the æsthetic sense and a stimulus and tonic to the ethical sense.

The essay makes no unit of impression, but undoubtedly the personality of the writer does; and this, I think, largely makes up, in such a writer as Emerson, for the want of inclosing design to which I have referred. The design that gives unity and relevancy to these isolated paragraphs is the personality of Emerson, his peculiar type and idiosyncrasy. This is the plan, the theme which these musical periods illustrate. The artist, says Goethe, "make what contortions he will, can only bring to light his own individuality." Of men of the Emersonian and Wordsworthian stamp, this is preëminently true; and it is this which finally interests us and gives the totality of impression in their works. The flavor of character is over all; the features of the man are stamped upon every word. From this point of view, much faultless and forcible writing — the writer always under the sway of Arnold's law of pure and flawless workmanship — is destitute of intrinsic style, because it is destitute of individuality. In the case of Emerson, the only new thing in the book is the man; this is the surprising discovery, but this makes all things new; we see the world through a new personal medium.

Everything Emerson wrote belongs to literature, and to literature in its highest and most serious mood. If not a great man of letters, then a great man speaking through letters, and delivering himself with a charm and a dignity few have equaled.

We cannot deny him literary honors, though we honor him for much more than his literary accomplishments. No more could a bird fly without wings than could Emerson's thought have reached and moved Arnold, in his early Oxford days, without rare qualities of literary style.

All Emerson's aspirations were toward greatness of character, greatness of wisdom, nobility of soul. Hence, in all his writings and speakings, the great man shines through and eclipses the great writer. The flavor of character is stronger than the flavor of letters, and dominates the pages.

If he is "the friend and aider of those who would live in the spirit," he is equally the friend and aider of those who would found a great state, a great literature, a great art. The spirit he brought to his task, and which he displayed throughout his life, is a stimulus and a support to all noble endeavor, of whatever kind or in whatever field.

Yet it is to be said that neither Emerson nor Carlyle was a typical literary man. They both had too great moral vehemence, or bent, to be the doctors and professors of mere literature for and of itself. They both belong to that class of writers who are not so much critics of life as feeders and reinforcers of life; who gather in from wide-lying realms, not always with nice judgment or wise selection, but always with bold, strong hands, much that nourishes and fertilizes the very roots of the tree

Igdrasil. Such writers were Emerson and Carlyle. Such a writer is *not* Mr. Arnold, though his function as pruner and cultivator of the tree is scarcely less in importance.

Disinterestedness is to be demanded of the critic, but the creative imagination may have free play within the limits of a strong intellectual bias. The charm and value of Darwin is his disinterestedness, but Darwin is a critic of the scheme of creation: he is interested only in finding and stating the largest truth, in outlining the theory that will cover the greatest multitude and the widest diversity of facts. But the charm and value of such a writer as Abraham Cowley, or Mr. Ruskin, or our Thoreau, is largely given by a peculiar moral and mental bias. It is Thoreau's stoicism and vehement partiality to nature that gives his page such a fillip and genial provocation. And what would Mr. Ruskin be without his delightful onesidedness and bright unreasonableness?

Few men eminent in literature have been free from some sort of bias. Arnold himself has the academic bias. There is in him a slight collegiate contemptuousness and aloofness which stands a little in the way of his doing full justice, say, to the nonconformist, and to the bereaved mortal who wants to marry his deceased wife's sister, and in the way of his full acceptance by his countrymen, to which he is justly entitled. Was he not also just a little *interested* in giving our pride in Emerson a fall, at least a shaking up? Milton is biased by his Puritanism; his "Paradise Lost" is the pageant or drama of the Puritan theology; but he is undoubtedly best as a poet when he forgets his Puritanism. Wordsworth has the didactic bias; his steed of the empyrean is yoked with another of much commoner clay. Carlyle's bias is an overweening partiality for heroes; he cuts all his cloth to this one pattern. Among our own writers, Bryant, Longfellow, Irving, have little or no bias; they are disinterested witnesses, but they are not men of the first order. Our younger corps of writers are free from bias, which is less a merit than their want of earnestness is a defect.

Arnold's view of Emerson as a poet is not entirely new, though perhaps it has never before been set forth in quite so telling and authoritative a form. The British literary journals have been in the habit of saying for years, whenever the subject was up, that Emerson was not a poet. An able London critic likened him to a Druid who wanders among the bards, and smites the harp with even more than bardic stress. And a poet on the usual terms we must admit Emerson was not. He truly had a druidical cast. His song is an incantation. Not a minstrel at the feast of life is he, but a chanter of runes at life's shrine. Arnold gave us the worst that could be said of Emerson as a poet, namely, that he lacked concreteness, sensuousness, and passion. Perhaps the best that can be said of him as a poet is that, notwithstanding these deficiencies, there is usually a poetic stress in his verse, a burden and an intensity of poetic appeal, that would be hard to match in any other poet. He had the eye and the ear of the poet preternaturally sharpened, but lacked the full poetic utterance. It would seem as if he besieged the Muses with all the more seriousness and eloquence because of the gifts that had been denied him. His verse is full of disembodied poetic values, of "melody born of melody." Compared with the other poets, he is like an essence compared to fruits or flowers. He pierced the symbol, he discarded the corporeal; his science savors of magic, his power of some mysterious occult force. Yet to say he is not a true poet implies too much; he does not stop short of the achievements of other poets, but goes beyond them. He would get rid of the bulk, the mass, and save the poetry; get rid of the concrete and catch the ideal; in other words, turn your mountain of carbon into diamonds.

As a rule, the qualities we miss from his verse he did not aim to put there; he did not himself value them in poetry. He knew the classic models were not for him. He valued only the memorable passages, the lightning strokes of genius, the line that

EMERSON AND CARLYLE

"Overleapt the horizon's edge,"

and

"Searched with Apollo's privilege."

He hung his verses in the wind: —

"All were winnowed through and through,
Five lines lasted sound and true;
Five were smelted in a pot
Than the South more fierce and hot;
These the siroc could not melt,
Fire their fiercer flaming felt,
And the meaning was more white
Than July's meridian light.
Sunshine cannot bleach the snow,
Nor time unmake what poets know.
Have you eyes to find the five
Which five hundred did survive?"

This was Emerson's method, — not to write a perfect poem, a poem that should be an inevitable whole, as Arnold would have him, but to write the perfect line, to set the imagination ablaze with a single verse, leaving the effects of form, of proportion, to be achieved by those who were equipped for it. His poetry is undoubtedly best when it is most concrete, as in the "Humble-Bee," "Rhodora," "Sea-Shore," "The Snow-Storm," "The Problem," "The Titmouse," and like poems, and poorest in "Woodnotes," "The Celestial Love," etc. "Unless the heart is shook," says Landor, "the gods thunder and stride in vain;" and the heart is seldom shook by Emerson's poetry. It has heat, but it is not that of English poetical literature, the heat of the blood, of the affections, the emotions ; but arises from the ecstasy of contemplation of the universality of the moral law.

It is hard to reconcile Arnold's criticism of Emerson's poetry with what many of us feel to be its beauty and value. It is irritating to Emersonians to be compelled to admit that his strain lacks any essential quality. I confess that I would rather have his poetry than all Milton, Cowper, Gray, Byron, and many others ever wrote, but doubtless in such a confession I am only pointing out my own limitations as a reader of the poets. This is the personal estimate which Arnold condemns. I see the grounds upon which Milton's poetry is considered greater, but I do not care for it, all the same. Emerson's poetry does not dilate me, as Wordsworth's does, because the human emotional element in it is weaker. It has not the same touch of nature that makes the whole world kin, the touch of commonalty heightened and vivified.

Whether we know it or not, we doubtless love Emerson all the more because he is not a legitimate poet or the usual man of letters, but an exceptional one. We do not love Shakespeare in the same way, because he is of no special and peculiar service to us as men and moral beings; he is not dear to any man, but generously beloved by all men. He is in the midst of the great currents of life and nature. 'T is the universal air, the universal water, we get here. But Emerson stands apart.

We go to him as we go to a fountain to drink, and to a fountain of peculiar virtues, a fountain that contains iron, or sulphur, or some other medicinal property. Hence, while to criticism Emerson is less than Gray or Milton, to us who need his moral and spiritual tonics he is more, vastly more. We live in a sick age, and he has saved the lives of many of us. So precious has his service been, so far beyond the reach of mere literature, that we are irritated, I say, when we hear the regular literary men placed above him. When I think of Emerson, I think of him as a man, not as an author; it was his rare and charming personality that healed us and kindled our love. When he died, it was not as a sweet singer, like Longfellow, who had gone silent ; but something precious and paternal had departed out of nature; a voice of hope and courage, and inspiration to all noble endeavor, had ceased to speak.

As a prose-writer, there is one note in Emerson which we get with the same emphasis and clearness in no other writer. I mean the heroic note, the note of manhood rising above the accidents of fortune and the tyranny of circumstances, the inspiration of courage and self-reliance. It is in Carlyle, but is often touched by his ill-humor. When

Teufelsdröckh fulminates his "Everlasting No" in
"Sartor Resartus," it rings out like a thunder-peal;
this is the wrath and invincibility of the hero at
bay. If, in Emerson's earlier essays, this note
seems to us now a little too pronounced, savoring
just a little of "tall talk," it did not seem so when
we first read them, but was as clear, and frank, and
sweet as the note of a bugle. Carlyle once defined
poetry as the "heroic of speech," a definition that
probably would not suit Mr. Arnold, but which
describes much of Emerson's verse, and many of
those brave sentences in his essays.

If in Addison the note is that of genial urbanity,
in Franklin that of worldly prudence ("There is a
flower of religion, a flower of honor, a flower of
chivalry," says Sainte-Beuve, "which must not be
required from Franklin"), in Bacon of large wisdom, in Pope of polished common-sense, in Arnold
himself the classical note or note of perfection, in
Emerson we come at once upon the chivalrous,
heroic attitude and temper. No scorn, no contempt,
no defiance, but a bright and cheerful confronting of
immense odds. In other writers there are words of
prudence, words of enlightenment, words of grave
counsel, words that divide one thing from another
like a blade, words of sympathy and love ; but in
Emerson more than in any other there are words
that are like banners leading to victory, symbolical,
inspiring, rallying, seconding, and pointing the way

to your best endeavor. "Self-trust," he says, "is the essence of heroism," and this martial note pulses through all his utterances. It is found in others, too, but it is the leading note in him. In others it is often the inspiration of conduct; in him it is the inspiration of morals.

The quality I refer to is in this passage from Marcus Aurelius: —

"Suppose that men kill thee — cut thee in pieces — curse thee. What, then, can these things do to prevent thy mind from remaining pure, wise, sober, just?"

It is in these lines from Beaumont and Fletcher's "Sea Voyage," quoted by Emerson himself: —

"*Julietta.* Why, slaves, 't is in our power to hang ye.
"*Master.* Very likely. 'T is in our power, then, to be hanged, and scorn ye."

It is the salt of this passage of another poet: —

"How beggarly appear arguments before a defiant deed!
How the floridness of the materials of cities shrivels be-
     fore a man's or woman's look!"

It is in the reply of the Spartan soldier who, when the threatening Persian told him their arrows would darken the sun, answered: "Very well, then; we will fight in the shade." Emerson sounds the same note throughout his essays, takes the same attitude toward circumstances, toward conventions, toward tradition, toward theological dogma, toward everything that would hamper and limit him. It shines in his famous boast: —

"Give me health and a day, and I will make the pomp of emperors ridiculous."

There is a glint of it in this passage, which might have been written to comfort John Brown, or to reassure a certain much-abused poet, had it not been before the fact, a prophecy and not a counsel: —

"Adhere to your own act, and congratulate yourself if you have done something strange and extravagant, and broken the monotony of a decorous age."

Here it takes another key: —

"If we dilate on beholding the Greek energy, the Roman pride, it is that we are already domesticating the same sentiment. Let us find room for this great guest in our small houses. The first step of worthiness will be to disabuse us of our superstitious associations with places and times, with number and size. Why should these words, Athenian, Roman, Asia, and England, so tingle in the ear? Where the heart is, there the muses, there the gods sojourn, and not in any geography of fame. Massachusetts, Connecticut River, and Boston Bay you think paltry places, and the ear loves names of foreign and classical topography. But here we are; and, if we will tarry a little, we may come to learn that here is best. See to it only that thyself is here, and art and nature, hope and

fate, friends, angels, and the Supreme Being shall
not be absent from the chamber where thou sittest."

Half the essays are to this tune. "Books," he
said, "are for nothing but to inspire;" and in writing
his own he had but one purpose in view: to be, as
Arnold so well says, "the friend and aider of those
who would live in the spirit,"—in the spirit of truth,
in the spirit of virtue, in the spirit of heroism.

The lecturer was unfortunate in what he said of
Emerson's "Titmouse." We do not learn, he said,
what his titmouse did for him; we are reduced to
guessing; he was not poet enough to tell us. But
the bird sounded the heroic note to the poet, and
inspired him with courage and hope when he was
about to succumb to the cold:—

> "Here was this atom in full breath,
>   Hurling defiance at vast death;
>
> .   .   .   .
>
> Henceforth I wear no stripe but thine;
> Ashes and jet all hues outshine.
>
> .   .   .   .
>
> I think old Cæsar must have heard
> In northern Gaul my dauntless bird,
> And, echoed in some frosty wold,
> Borrowed thy battle-numbers bold.
>
> .   .   .   .
>
> *Pæan! Veni, vidi, vici.*"

It is one of Emerson's most characteristic poems.
Burns, the speaker said, would have handled the

subject differently, thinking probably of Burns's "Mouse." Certainly he would. He was pitched in a different key. The misfortunes of his mouse touched his sympathy and love, appealed to his human tenderness, and called up the vision of his own hard lot. Each poet gives us the sentiment proper to him; the heroic from Emerson, the human from Burns. The lecturer was right in saying that the secret of Emerson's influence is his temper, but it is not merely his good temper, his cheerfulness, hopefulness, benevolence. These he shared with the mass of his countrymen. The American temperament is sanguine and turns confidently to the future. But it is again his heroic temper, his faith in "the ideal tendencies," in the value of personal force and character, in the grandeur of the present moment, the present opportunity; a temper he shares with but few, but shares, say, with his friend and master, Carlyle: —

"One equal temper of heroic hearts;"

and more especially in Carlyle's case,

"Made weak by time and fate, but strong in will
To strive, to seek, to find, and not to yield."

It has long been clear to me that Carlyle and Emerson were in many important respects closely akin, notwithstanding the wrath and melancholy of the one, and the serenity and hopefulness of the other. Their main ground of kinship is the heroic sentiment which they share in common. Their effects upon the mind are essentially the same: both have the "tart cathartic virtue" of courage and self-reliance; both nourish character and spur genius. Carlyle does not communicate the gloom he feels; 't is the most tonic despair to be found in literature. There is a kind of felicity in it. For one thing, it sprang from no personal disappointment or selfishness. It always has the heroic tinge. In a letter to Emerson he refers to it as a "kind of imperial sorrow that is almost like felicity, — so completely and composedly wretched, one is equal to the very gods." His wretchedness was a kind of *sorrow;* that is always its saving feature. One's unhappiness may be selfish and ignoble, or it may be noble and inspiring; all depends upon the sentiment from which it springs. Men selfishly wretched never laugh, except in derision. Carlyle was a man of sorrow, and sorrow springs from sympathy and love. A sorrowing man is a loving man. His is the Old World sorrow, the inheritance of ages, the grief of justice and retribution over the accumulated wrongs and sufferings of centuries. In him it became a kind of poetic sentiment, a fertile leaf-mould that issued at last in positive verdure and bloom. Not happiness, but a kind of blessedness, he aspired to, the satisfaction of suffering in well-doing. How he loves all the battling, struggling, heroic souls!

Whenever he comes upon one such in his histories, no matter how obscure, he turns aside to lay a wreath upon his tomb. It was his own glory that he never flinched; that his despair only nerved him to work the harder; the thicker the gloom, the more his light shone. Hope and heart never left him; they were of the unquenchable, the inextinguishable kind, like those ragged jets of flame the traveler used to see above the oil wells or gas wells in Pennsylvania, which the wildest tempest could not blow out, so tenaciously and desperately did the flame cling.

Carlyle's lamentations are loud; a little of his own doctrine of silence would have come in well here. What he said of Voltaire the world is bound to say of himself: "Truly M. de Voltaire had a talent for speech, but lamentably wanted that of silence." But he worked like a Hercules. He does not charm the demons away like Emerson, but he defies them. Emerson wins them over, but Carlyle explodes them with their own sulphur. Each man rendered his age and country a signal service, and to rule them out of the company of the great authors is to rob that company of the two names of this century it can least afford to lose.

GILBERT WHITE'S BOOK

I WAS moved to take down my White's "Selborne" and examine it again for the source of the delight I had had in it, on hearing a distinguished literary man, the late Richard Grant White, say it was a book he could not read with any degree of pleasure: to him its pages were a bare record of uninteresting facts. It was not because he felt no interest in or sympathy with the kind of literature to which White's "Selborne" belongs, for he confessed a liking for certain other writers in this field, but because both White's matter and manner were void of interest to him. The book was doubtless pitched in too low a key for him: it was tame and commonplace, like the country itself. There is indeed something a little disappointing in White's book when one takes it up for the first time, with his mind full of its great fame. It is not seasoned quite up to the modern taste. White is content that the facts of nature should be just what they are; his concern alone is to see them just as they are. When I myself first looked into his book, many years ago, I found nothing in it that attracted me, and so passed it by. Later it fell into my hands, when I felt its charm and value at once. Indeed, the work of the Selborne naturalist belongs to the class of books that one must discover for himself : their quality is not patent ; he that runs may not read them. Like certain fruits, they leave a lingering flavor in the mouth that is much better than the first taste promised. In some congenial mood or lucky moment you find them out. I remember I had the little book of Essays of Abraham Cowley some years before I succeeded in reading it. One summer day I chanced to take it with me on my walk to the woods, and at the foot of a waterfall in a very secluded place I suddenly discovered that the essays had a quality and a charm that I had never suspected they possessed. The book was the fruit of a certain privacy and seclusion from the world, and it required in the reader the frame of mind which these beget in order to enter fully into it. I suspect that some such auspicious moment or preparation is necessary to a full appreciation of White's letters. It is necessary, in the first place, that you be a born countryman, capable of a certain fellowship and intimacy with your brute neighbors and with the various shows of rural nature. Then a quiet, even tenor of life, such as can be had only in the country, is also necessary, — a way of life that goes slow, and lingers upon the impression of the moment, and returns to it again and again, that

Gilbert White's House, Selborne

makes much of little things, and is closely observant
of the face of the day and of the landscape, and
into which the disturbing elements of the great
hurly-burly outside world do not enter. Being thus
surrounded and thus inclined, in the fall, when you
first build a fire in your grate and begin to feel
again like browsing along the old paths, open
White's "Selborne," and read a chapter here and
there, and bend your ear attentively to his quiet,
cheerful, but earnest talk. Each letter shall seem
addressed to you personally with news from the
fields and byways you so lately visited. The pas-
toral quiet and sweetness and harmony of the English landscape pervade them all, with just that tinge
of reminiscence, that flavor of human sympathy and
human absorption, that English fields suggest. The
style is like a rich, tender sward, simple and unob-
trusive, with scarcely a flower of rhetoric anywhere,
but very pleasing and effective and entirely ade-
quate: it is nature and art perfectly married, each
seconding the other. Its brevity, its directness, its
simplicity, its dealings with familiar and near-at-
hand objects, shows, occurrences, make it a book
which never sates and never tires the reader. It
is little more than an appetizer, but as such it takes
high rank. As a stimulus and spur to the study
of natural history, it has no doubt had more influence than any other work of the century. Its merits
in this direction alone would perhaps account for

its success. But, while it has other merits, and great ones, it has been a fortunate book: it has had little competition; it has had the wind always with it, so to speak. It furnished a staple the demand for which was always steady and the supply small. There was no other book of any merit like it for nearly a hundred years. It contains a great deal of good natural history and acute observations upon various rural subjects, put up in a cheap and portable form. The contemporary works of Pennant are voluminous and costly, — heavy sailing-craft only, that come to port in the great libraries, while this is a nimble, light-draught vessel that has found a harbor on nearly every man's book-shelf.

Hence we say that while it is not one of the great books, it is one of the very *real* books, one of the very *live* books, and has met and supplied a tangible want in the English reading world. It does not appeal to a large class of readers, and yet no library is complete without it. It is valuable as a storehouse of facts, it is valuable as a treatise on the art of observing things, and it is valuable for its sweetness and charm of style.

What an equable, harmonious, and gracious spirit and temper pervade the book, and withal what an air of summer-day leisure and sequestration! The great world is far off. Its sound is less than the distant rumble of a wagon heard in the midst of the fields. The privacy and preoccupation of the author are like those of the bird building her nest, or of the bee gathering her sweets. He was eager for news, but it was only for news from the earth and the air, or from the dumb life about him. Yet it would not be safe to affirm that White was not an interested and sympathetic spectator of the events of his time, like other men, for doubtless he was. There is no evidence that he was anything like the petulant recluse and man-hater that our own Thoreau at times was. He had the wide, generous eye, and his love of nature was not in any sense a running away from the world. But he was not the historian of his time, nor even of his own moods and fancies, but the chronicler of the unobserved life of nature about him; and as such he attained a pure result. And this is one secret of his keeping qualities, — a pure result, untainted and unrefracted by any peculiarity of the medium through which it came. Mankind, in the long run, cares less what you think, unless your plummet goes very deep, than what you feel, and are, and experience. White valued his facts for what they were, not for any double meaning he could wring out of them, or any airy structure he could build upon them. He loved the bird, or the animal, or a walk in the fields, directly and for its own sake, and his book makes a distinct impression, like any of the creatures or any of the phases and products of nature of which it treats. The perennial and essential quality in literature or art is something as simple as water or milk, or as the oxygen of the air: it does not come from afar; it is more common and familiar than we are apt to think. One may not say dogmatically that it is this or that, but I think it safe to say that it is inseparable from perfect seriousness and singleness of purpose. This singleness and seriousness of purpose White had. He is as honest and direct as the rain or the wind. No levity, no seeing double, no intellectual astigmatism, no make-believe, no spinning of webs, hardly any conscious humor, no overripe sentiment, but a steady effort and purpose to see and record the simple fact. It is not more what he has put into his book than what he has kept out of it that has made it keep a hundred years. Carlyle says of a certain celebrated Frenchman, that he was always at the top less by power of swimming than by lightness in floating. In no disparaging sense is this true of White's "Selborne." It has an inherent principle of buoyancy like a bird. It is a light book in the best sense. It makes no severe demand upon the reader's time or attention. It is as easy reading as the letters of a friend. The epistolary form of the chapters — a form that lends itself so readily, almost inevitably, to directness and simplicity of statement — is no doubt one secret of the book's charm. Dullness in private letters is perhaps rarer than dullness in any other species of writing. Plenty of persons write fresh and entertaining letters who are lead itself in the essay or the sermon. White is less pleasing in his "Observations of Nature" than in his letters. It is a great matter to have a fair and definite mark to aim at, and a good reason for obtruding the personal pronoun. White was the type of the true observer. He had the alert, open sense, the genial, hospitable habit of mind, the healthful objectivity and receptivity, that at once placed him in right relations with outward nature. He had great curiosity and genuine enthusiasm, and permitted no moods, or humors, or bias, or what not, to stand between him and what he saw. His mind transmitted clearly; the image is exact. To be a good observer is not merely to see things: it is to see them in their relations and bearings; it is to separate one thing from another, the wheat from the chaff, the significant from the unimportant. The sagacity of the hound is in his scent, the skill of the musician seems in his hands and fingers, the mind of the observer is in his eye. To untrained perceptions the color of the clouds is this or that, gray, or blue, or drab; the artist picks out the primary tints, the separate colors of which this hue is composed. In like manner the true observer, the true eye-poet or analyst, disentangles the facts and threads of meaning of the dumb life about him, and gives you a distinct impression. It is true that White m   a business of observing. For more than forty years he went out daily to take note of what was going on in his open-air parish. He knew his ground by heart, and every new move at once caught his eye. If a new bird appeared upon the scene, he was sure to be on hand to take note of it ; or if a swallow lingered a little later than usual, or came a day or two earlier, the fact did not escape him. The pine grosbeak is a rare visitant in England, as it is in the United States, yet if one came, it was pretty sure to report to White at an early day.

The hoopoe is also a rare bird here ; but one summer a pair took up their abode in an ornamental piece of ground that joined White's garden. One can imagine how eagerly he watched them. "They used to march about in a stately manner," he says, "feeding in the walks many times a day, and seemed disposed to breed in my outlet, but were frightened and persecuted by idle boys, who would never let them be at rest." The grasshopper-lark is one of the shyest of British birds, and one of the most baffling to the observer. It creeps around under the thorns and bushes and in the bottom of the hedge-rows, like a mouse or a weasel. Its note or song was thought to proceed from a grasshopper; and White says the country people laugh when told it is a bird. But the sharp-eyed curate could not be baffled : he would watch the bird till he saw it in the very act. His eye was not only quick, it was patient and tenacious, and would not let go till it had the secret. He saw the fern-owl feed itself while on the wing; he saw swallows feed their young in the air, which few people have perhaps ever seen. He timed the white owls that nested under the eaves of his church, and, with watch in hand, found that one or the other of them returned about every five minutes with food for the young. They did not proceed directly to the nest, but always perched upon the roof of the chancel first. He quickly saw what this was for: it was to shift the mouse from the claws to the bill, that their feet might be free to aid them in climbing to the nest. His observation is often of the minutest character. "When redstarts shake their tails," he says, "they move them horizontally, as dogs do when they fawn; the tail of a wagtail when in motion bobs up and down like that of a jaded horse." "Most birds drink sipping at intervals; but pigeons take a long-continued draught, like quadrupeds." When he saw the stilt-plover, he observed at once that it had no back toe, and must therefore be a bad walker. "Without that steady prop to support its steps, it must be liable, in speculation, to perpetual vacillations, and seldom able to preserve the true centre of gravity." There is a sly, humorous twinkle in this passage that our author seldom indulges in.

White's interest and curiosity in every phase of natural history were so lively, and his habit of mind was so frank and open, that much came in his way to record that would otherwise have been passed by. His neighbor had a hog which he kept to an advanced age, and our curate writes to Mr. Barrington one of his characteristic letters about it. "The natural term of a hog's life," he begins, "is little known, and the reason is plain, — because it is neither profitable nor convenient to keep that turbulent animal to the full extent of its time; however, my neighbor, a man of substance, who had no occasion to study every little advantage to a nicety, kept an half-bred Bantam sow, who was as thick as she was long, and whose belly swept on the ground, till she was advanced to her seventeenth year, at which period she showed some tokens of age by the decay of her teeth and the decline of her fertility." Two or three of his most charming letters are devoted to the "old family tortoise." What a clear and vivid impression we get of the creature! and what a lively interest we feel in its stupid ways! "No part of its behavior," says White, "ever struck me more than the extreme timidity it always expresses with regard to rain ; for, though it has a shell that would secure it against the wheel of a loaded cart, yet does it discover as much solicitude about rain as a lady dressed in all her best attire, shuffling away on the first sprinklings and running its head up in a corner." The old tortoise begins to dig a hole in the ground to go into winter quarters early in November. "It scrapes out the ground with its fore-feet," says the historian, "and throws it up over its back with its hind; but the motion of its legs is ridiculously slow, little exceeding the hour-hand of a clock." "This creature not only goes under the earth from the middle of November to the middle of April, but sleeps great part of the summer; for it goes to bed in the longest days at four in the afternoon, and often does not stir in the morning till late. Besides, it retires to rest for every shower, and does not move at all in wet days." Though so stupid and sleepy most of the time, "yet there is a season of the year (usually the beginning of June) when his exertions are remarkable. He then walks on tiptoe, and is stirring by five in the morning, and, traversing the garden, examines every wicket and interstice in the fences, through which he will escape, if possible, and often has eluded the care of the gardener and wandered to some distant field. The motives that impel him to undertake these rambles seem to be of the amorous kind; his fancy then becomes intent on sexual attachments, which transport him beyond his usual gravity and induce him to forget for a time his ordinary solemn deportment."

Not less graphic and interesting is his account of the idiot boy who had a passion for bees and honey, — was, in fact, a veritable bee-eater, seeking the bees in the field and about the hives, and, as he ran about, making a humming noise with his lips that resembled the buzzing of bees. Nothing, in fact, escaped White's attention, and his interest in things is so sane and natural, and at the same time so lively, that his pages never become obsolete.

The American reader of his book will hardly fail to give many of his notes and observations an application at home, and to see wherein our own familiar natural history agrees with or differs from that of the mother country. The toad appears to be a common reptile in England, yet White confessed his ignorance of its manner of propagation, — whether it laid eggs or brought forth its young alive, — and could get no light from the authorities of his time upon the subject. But the fact with regard to frogs, he said, was notorious to everybody. With us, the fact with regard to toads is just as obvious. Their spawning habits may be noticed in the spring in every marsh and roadside pool, the large, sedate, grandmotherly female toad bearing the pert, dapper little male, looking like her ten-year-old grandson, upon her back. It is apparently a copartnership between a dwarf and a giant. When the female is disturbed, she plunges to the bottom of the pool, and buries herself in the mud, carrying the clinging male with her, as if he was a very slight appendage indeed. The chain of eggs that trails behind, and that may be many yards in length, looks like a knitted black yarn in a cord of transparent jelly. White says of the British frogs, that as soon as they have passed out of the tadpole state they take to the land, and that at times the lanes, paths, and fields swarm with myriads of them on their travels. A similar phenomenon may be witnessed in this country, except that the tiny travelers are toads, and not frogs, and they are not migrating, but are out only when it rains, and then to wet their jackets. I have never seen them except along the highway upon gravelly hills in early summer. They are then scarcely as large as bumblebees.

White repeatedly speaks of the house swallow, which corresponds to our barn swallow, as a fine songster. In soft, sunny weather, he says, it sings both perching and flying. If this is so, it is a point in favor of the British bird. Our swallow is not a songster; and yet the epithet which Virgil applies to the swallow — *garrula* — fits our bird. It twitters and squeaks and calls; but is that singing? Our cliff swallow does the same; and yet White says the English martin, or martlet, which is like our bird, is not a songster, though it twitters in a pretty, inward, soft manner in its nest. Again, the swift, which answers to our chimney swallow, he says, has only a harsh, screaming note or two. But our swift has a very pretty chippering note or call, which it indulges in on the wing, and which approaches very nearly to a song. On the whole,

I conclude from White's account that the common
European swallow has more music in him than ours
has, while our swift and martin are more musical
than the corresponding species in that country.
There is this marked difference between the habits
of the birds in the two hemispheres : the swallow
that in Europe builds in chimneys, and is called the
house or chimney swallow, in this country builds in
barns and other outhouses, and is called the barn
swallow; while the swift, which builds in chimneys
here, and uses as material small twigs gathered from
the tops of dry trees, in England builds in cran-
nies of castles and towers and steeples, and uses for
material dry grasses and feathers, — which, however, it seems to gather on the wing, as our bird
does its twigs.

White says that birds that build on the ground
do not make much of their nests, — that is, I suppose, are not much attached to them.   But this
observation would not hold in this country.   Our
song sparrow and field sparrow, our bobolink, and
oven-bird, and chewink, and brown thrasher, and
Canada warbler, show as strong an attachment for
their nests as do the tree-builders, and use as many
arts to decoy the intruder away from them.   They
build quite as elaborate nests, too; which does not
seem to be the case with ground-builders in Europe.
There are few finer and neater architects among the
birds than our song sparrow and snowbird.

Chewink

Rudy Agassiz Gruelle

White lays it down "as a maxim in ornithology that as long as there is any incubation going on there is music." This is true of our birds also : they continue in song until the young are hatched. But the converse of the proposition is not true, that there is incubation as long as there is music. Certain species continue in song long after the last brood has flown. I am convinced that more birds continue in song in late summer and in early autumn in this country than in England.

The main features of White's country are apparently but little changed since his time. The Hanger is there, with its noble beeches, and a large part of Wolmer Forest still remains. I passed two rainy days and one night at Selborne in June, 1882. At the hotel where I stayed, a copy of White's book could not be produced. The village is small, compact, and humble. The postman handed me my letters upon the street without remark, as if I was the only stranger in the place, — which was probably true. The soil of that part of England is a heavy, greasy clay. On the steepest part of the Hanger the boys ride or slide down the hill in summer. The turf is removed, and the slippery clay is a fair substitute for ice. White's house had been recently much changed. It stands in the midst of the village, close to the street, and not amid spacious grounds, as one has been led to believe. I looked a long time for his tomb amid the graves that surrounded the old church, and finally found a plain slab with " G. W." upon it, and that was all. There was no mark that indicated that the grave was more frequently visited than any other. The church is essentially the same as in White's time, and the immense yew that stands near the entrance must date back several hundred years. The yew is a striking-looking tree. In this country the species is represented by a low, reclining bush, which reaches out laterally, with but a slight tendency upward. In England the lateral tendency of growth is still very marked, the trunk being short and squat, and by its ridgy, corrugated character looking more like a bundle or sheaf of smaller trees than like a single bole.

Thus far White stands alone among English writers in his field. Much pleasant literature has of late years been inspired by nature-studies in Great Britain, but the new books have not quite the sweetness and charm, not quite the sincerity, of that of the Selborne parson.

VII

A MALFORMED GIANT[1]

DE QUINCEY somewhere remarks that the Roman mind was great in the presence of man, never in the presence of nature. I am not going to undertake to say whether or not this observation is wholly true. Undoubtedly there is truth in it. I remember Gibbon says that to the Romans the ocean was an object of terror rather than of curiosity, and that that warlike people was never "actuated by the enterprising spirit which had prompted the navigators of Tyre, of Carthage, and even of Marseilles to enlarge the bounds of the world, and to explore the most remote coasts of the ocean." But empire upon the land came easy to the Roman. He was great in war, in government, in jurisprudence, and in the administration of all human affairs.

[1] Perhaps I ought to apologize to my reader for the polemical tone of the latter part of this essay. It was written many years ago in reply to an able critic, the late William D. O'Connor, who had resented my epithet of "mad-dog" as applied to Victor Hugo's nature, and I find it impossible to change it now. As a protest against the glaring vice of Hugo's art I think it well enough; I would only change its vehement and controversial tone and temper.

De Quincey's distinction came to my mind in meditating upon Victor Hugo. Here, I said, is a great man, unquestionably a great man, who shows to least advantage in his dealings with nature. He seems to feel something of the Roman dread and horror in the presence of the ocean. Great in dealing with social problems or historical events, great in describing Waterloo, or the sewers of Paris, or Paris itself, tremendous in the realism of his characters, in the presence of storms or tempests, or of any phase of elemental nature, his imagination runs away with him. His nature is a kind of mad-dog nature, and the physical universe, in his handling of it, seems smitten with hydrophobia. The continence, the moderation, the self-denial which the Anglo-Saxon temperament loves, and which characterizes nearly all first-class poets and artists, are nowhere to be found. If he mentions the song of the skylark, he must call upon the infinite and the immensities to bear witness. One fully understands what Heine means when he speaks of Hugo's " huge and tasteless excrescences." Yet it is impossible not to feel the man's power even in the poorest translation of his books. He is about the only writer of his country who impresses one as a man who rises above the *literature*, whose love of letters is dominated by his love of country, his love of man, his love of liberty and right, — a fact which makes him a great moral and political force aside from his influence in the region of letters. There is somewhat aboriginal and elemental in him, as in all first-class men. The bare conception of "The Man who Laughs" is tremendous. Only the first order of minds can conjure up such material and deal with such a *motif*. It is like the granite rock. But oh the absurdities and anachronisms in the working of it up! "The Toilers," too, faces realities of the largest kind, but there are things in it which, as Robert Louis Stevenson well says, simply make the reader cover his face with his hands, the artistic falsehoods are so glaring. The description of the storm which overtakes Gilliat just as his task is about finished resembles the work of the great artists about as nearly as a nightmare resembles the reality. Yet in all these romances everything is large, elemental ; no hair-splitting, nothing petty or over-refined. It is the work of a giant, but one malformed. Hugo at once strikes a louder, stronger key than any of his contemporaries. His voice rises above all others, and is as full of cheer and hope as it is full of denunciation and wrath. He was like dynamite and giant powder, which make themselves heard and felt afar. He had no repose, and this is one reason why he is so irritating to the English mind. Another reason is his want of self-restraint. As a literary artist he out-Herods Herod. In the torrent, tempest, and whirlwind of his passion, all goes by the board. "The modesty of nature," which Hamlet laid such stress upon in his address to the players, is not only "o'erstepped," it is outrageously insulted. Probably never before in the history of literature has a master spirit cut such fantastic tricks before the high heaven of literary art. He illustrates in his field excesses and violences as great as those which have marked the history of the French people. His offenses against good taste, against one's sense of fitness and proportion, are, in their way, on a par with the monstrous doings of the French Revolution. The writer shocks one's artistic perceptions, as the people shock one's reason and humanity. And in both cases it was rebellion run mad. The revolt of the people against the authority of the state and of the priests became frenzy, and the revolt of Hugo against the classic standards became rodomontade. He was a romanticist, which he construed to mean just the contrary of the classicist. One law of Greek art and of Greek life was, nothing in excess, — a wise measure in all things; therefore Hugo piles on the agony: the classic authors were calm, they avoided everything sensational, all undue emphasis; therefore will Hugo rave and be sensational: they cultivated a sobriety and temperance which instinctively avoided everything that was calculated to weaken an impression; therefore does the Frenchman give free rein to his rhetoric and ride roughshod over all such tame consideration. Relevancy, harmony

of parts, unity of impression, — these are some of
the excellences of the classics; but "Les Misérables," with all its power and effectiveness, is like
a man with elephantiasis in some of his members.
When about a third of it is cut away, the story has
some unity. Where the classics are dramatic, Hugo
is melodramatic, — note Gilliat in "The Toilers"
seating himself upon the shore to be drowned by the
tide, and his head disappearing under the water at
the moment the sloop he is watching drops behind
the horizon. Where the old writers are simple, he
is sensational. The Anglo-Saxon mind, and every
other normal and healthful type of mind, is classical in this: it loves proportion, restraint, self-denial,
and has a lively sense of the fitness of things; does
not like any trifling with the centre of gravity, and
keeps close to the simple truth. Let a man fire
hot shot if he will, but let him keep his own guns
cool. In nearly all Victor Hugo's political tracts
and manifestoes the gun is hotter than the shot
which it throws, and we are more concerned for the
writer than we are for his enemy. He will spur
his earnestness until it becomes frenzy, and his
rhetoric until it becomes rodomontade. Note his
manifesto to the Prussians during the siege of Paris.
To see him rending his flesh, livid with rage and
almost foaming at the mouth, read certain pages in
his "Napoleon the Little;" or to see him again,
under a different pressure, beating the air wildly,

and goading his imagination after his climax is reached, like a rider burying his rowel into his steed after the poor beast has long done its best, read the concluding parts of his description of the battle of Waterloo, or the last stages of the storm that overtakes Gilliat in "The Toilers," or the threefold agony of the rhetoric of a similar description in "The Man who Laughs" (the machine that grins, a friend says). To be great in the presence of nature, to be great in any presence, is to stand firmly on your feet, to use all gently, and in the very torrent, tempest, and (as I may say) whirlwind of your passion, acquire and beget a temperance that will give it smoothness. In the case of Victor Hugo, when the pressure of his passion mounts to a certain pitch, he invariably flies from his orbit, and from being planetary, as Æschylus and Shakespeare always are, becomes cometary and lawless, losing fervor in fury and reason in riot. He would have every storm a cyclone, every fish a monster, every clown a gnome, a medusa; and if they are not so, it is not his fault. He "pushes the passions till the bond of nature snaps and all the furies come screeching in." Let me explain myself further. Close alongside of the sphere of the normal lies the sphere of the abnormal; of the sane, lies the insane; of pleasure, lies disgust; of cohesion, lies dissolution; of the grotesque, lies the hideous; of the sublime, lies the ridiculous; of power, lies plethora; of sense, lies twaddle. Take but a step sometimes and you pass from one to the other, from a shout to a scream, from the heroic to the vainglorious. Victor Hugo, in his imaginative flights, is forever hovering about this dividing line, fascinated, spellbound by what lies beyond, and in his reachings after it outraging the "modesty of nature" till the very soul blushes. It would seem as if he loved the unnatural simply because it is the unnatural, and the malformed simply because it is the malformed. He loves to push the normal till it becomes the abnormal, the dramatic till it becomes the melodramatic, the intense till it becomes the hysterical; he loves to push anger, jealousy, remorse, grief, till the bond snaps and Termagant is overdone. His characters rave, gnash, rend their hair, froth at the mouth, and even die in paroxysms of passion. No doubt, in the opinion of Victor Hugoites like Swinburne, there is no reason why their eyes should not leap from their sockets, their flesh wither on their bones, or serpents hiss from their ears, nose, and mouth, if the "imperial fantasy" of the novelist orders it. I am not now thinking of his poems, some of which I regard as truly great, but of his leading characteristics as a novelist; of "Bug-Jargal" and "Notre Dame." How fares the modesty of nature in these volumes? The former is not so well known, but what shall we say of the latter? Let us examine it a little, since this is one of his masterpieces. As a work of art, what is it a faithful transcript of ? It is full of monstrosities, both moral and physical, full of distorted passions, unhallowed lusts, fiendish brutality, diabolical ravings, writhing agonies, hideous grimaces, sepulchral wailings, — full of all manner of underground horrors and aboveground abominations. It is a carnival of the loathsome. If, underneath these things, and inclosing them, one recognized the great remedial forces of nature, or the compensations of time and history, there would be some refuge, some escape. But the earth is rotten, the sunshine pestiferous, the waters stygian, Paris a den of cutthroats and thieves, love is lechery, and religion death. This fact alone quashes all minor excellence. No work is permissible that flies in the teeth of the established order of the universe. It is the business of the artist, above all else, to preserve the balance of things. Creation is not by one element alone. Fire alone consumes; earth, air, water, are also necessary.

In struggling through the blistering, arid wastes of Hysteria that abound in this novel, one remembers with profound emotion the silence of Ajax in Hell, and sees with Longinus that it was more impressive than anything he could have said ; or the soldier of Waterloo, who, when asked to surrender in that crater of fire and death, could find but one word in which to express his scorn and defiance, and that a word of filth, not permissible in print. (Is there any doubt about how the same spirit would greet Hugo's grand burst over the circumstances?)

The action of the story of "Notre Dame" perhaps culminates when the monster Quasimodo defends the church of Notre Dame against the midnight assault of about six thousand Truands — the nocturnal human vermin of Paris during the Middle Ages — composed of thieves, harlots, murderers, beggars, gypsies, — a reeking, fetid, scrofulous, chaotic mass, that smelled to heaven. As they surge about the building in the darkness, the Hunchback hurls upon them from a height of nearly two hundred feet, first a huge beam, that spatters them in fragments about; then bricks, stones, rocks, that bury themselves in their heads. Finally, not being able to make an impression on this nightmare of a mob, he kindles a huge fire in one of the towers and piles upon it sheets of lead, and presently two huge gutters vomit upon the assailants a shower of molten metal which is represented as burning them to cinders. In any less vivid imagination than Victor Hugo's, molten lead, after running some distance over stone gutters and falling one hundred and eighty feet through a cool atmosphere, would have resulted in a shower of bullets, — to say nothing of its burning people to cinders.

But this is, no doubt, an instance in which

he exercises the prerogative of his "imperial fantasy."

In the same assault a mere youth heavily laden with armor is represented as bringing with celerity a ladder which must have been seventy feet long, and not only carrying it but placing it in position. Quite a feat for a mere youth, what indeed ten men could not do (allowing that a single ladder of that length was ever made, which of course is absurd), but a mere straw to the imperial fantasy of Victor Hugo. It was the same imperial fantasy, no doubt, that kept the naked feet, to say nothing of his half-clad body, of the boy Gwynplaine from freezing in that four or six hours' ramble over the Portland hills through the snow and bitter cold, now on the ice, now in the water, now floundering through drifts, his rags stiff, the icy edges chafing the flesh till the blood comes (?). The same fantastic sovereignty causes the cyclone in the northern hemisphere to revolve in the direction of the hands of a watch, and sends an unencumbered sailor, when he leaps from a sinking wreck to swim to a distant rock, several fathoms under water, and sets him groping around on the submarine ledges before he rises to the surface in order that the apocryphal devil-fish may get hold of him.

But to continue the review of "Notre Dame." In the concluding chapters of this novel the author indulges to the utmost his love for the monstrous and abnormal exhibitions of the human passions, and there is no escape ; not even does the stern visage of Justice loom above the scene, or the grander visage of Destiny.

In the distance a man ascends a ladder to a permanent gibbet, carrying a female figure on his shoulder, — a young girl clad in white. The noose is adjusted, the ladder kicked away, and the delicate form is launched into the air with the figure of a man squatted upon its shoulders.

At this moment, in the foreground, on one of the towers of Notre Dame, a priest who is contemplating the scene with outstretched neck, starting eyeballs, and livid visage, being driven to the verge of insanity by sheer brutal lust for the girl, but thwarted in his designs by her horror of himself and her love for another, is suddenly set upon from behind by the enraged Hunchback, who it seems is also in love with the girl, and precipitated over the balustrade into the abyss. But the gutter arrests his fall, and he clings to it with desperate grip.

Here Hugo dallies with him and gloats over him. He is suspended two hundred feet above the pavement, and cannot long maintain his hold. It is a startling situation, and Hugo loves startling situations. He contemplates him panting, perspiring, his nails bleeding against the stones, his knees grazing the wall, the lead pipe gradually yielding, his strength failing, his hands slipping, his vitals freezing, till the inevitable moment comes, and he falls through the void to the earth beneath. We repeat that there would be no objection to all this if it contained food for the imagination, if it opened any ideal depths in the mind, or was relieved by any background; but, excepting that the verbal workmanship is vastly better, it ranks no higher as art than the blood-and-thunder stories of the weekly novelette.

If a man is drawn into the maelstrom, or falls into a volcano, or is lost at sea, or goes down in battle, or meets suffering and death in a heroic manner, there is room for the imagination to work; but art would have little interest in a man being sawed in two, or roasted alive, or crushed under a weight, or dangling at the end of a rope. If the "Prometheus" of Æschylus had nothing to recommend it but the aspect of physical torture which it depicts, however vividly painted, it would at once lose its value as a work of art.

There is therefore this final remark to be made upon the element of the hideous and the monstrous that figures so largely in Victor Hugo's novels, and that is this: It has little or no artistic value, because it has little or no interest to the imagination. When employed by the old artists and poets, these things are so charged and surcharged with meaning and power that the literal import is lost sight of, and the mind breathes a higher atmosphere.

A MALFORMED GIANT

Hugo's novels are marked by a feverish, preternatural intensity, not so much good, human, soulshaking emotion as a sort of psychological typhoon and hurricane that means death to every green thing and to every sane impulse. I am aware that a microscopical examination of his works reveals many fine passages, green spots, idyllic touches here and there (but even in these I can smell the sulphur), but to say they are characteristic of him is as absurd as it would be to say that humor is characteristic of him because he made a "machine that grins."

The Bishop in "Les Misérables" is perhaps Hugo's most serious attempt to paint (for he does not create) a lofty character. And what is the Bishop's attitude toward the All-mother? "The universe appeared to him like a vast disease," for aught I know as if "smitten with hydrophobia." His tenderness toward nature is so excessive as to become silliness. "One day he received a sprain rather than crush an ant." "One morning he was in his garden and thought himself alone, but his sister was walking behind him : all at once he stopped and looked at something on the ground ; it was a large, black, hairy, horrible spider. His sister heard him say: 'Poor thing! it is not his fault.'" A galley slave whom he had hospitably fed and lodged in his house makes off in the night with his silver. In the morning he is walking in the garden again, when his "women folks" make the discovery and raise the alarm; but, so far from sharing in the surprise or the indignation which was quite proper on the occasion, he thinks only of a little flower that the man had crushed in passing out, and bends over it with a look of sadness and pity. There may be persons to whom this sort of thing is impressive and grand, but for my part I cannot see how it can ever be possible to one having a genuine feeling or appreciation of nature.

The mighty poet does not recreate nature in any radical sense. He redistributes, remoulds, remarries, when occasion requires, always bearing in mind the almighty edict, "Thus far shalt thou go and no farther." And it is the final test and glory of his work that though vast and imposing, it falls easily within the scope of the natural universal.

VIII

BRIEF ESSAYS

I

THE BIOLOGIST'S TREE OF LIFE

ONE of the most helpful and satisfactory conceptions of modern biological science is the conception of the animal life of the globe under the image of a tree, — a tree which has its root and trunk in the remote past, and its outermost twigs and branches in our own day ; and, moreover, a tree which has attained its growth, which has reached its maturity, and whose history in the far future must be marked by a slow decline. This is the Tree of Life of the evolutionist, and affords the key to the natural classification of the animal kingdom as taught by Darwin and others, and as opposed to the artificial or arbitrary classification of Cuvier and the older naturalists. This tree first emerges into view in the Silurian age, probably not less than fifty million years ago, and emerges as a pretty well-developed tree, that is, as having many branches. Its trunk is beyond our ken, hidden in still more remote ages. No fossils have been found in rocks older than the Silurian. But if evolution is true, it is pretty certain that there must have been life on the globe long before that date. Our tree must have started as a single shoot, but this single stem, our first parent form, has not been found. The biologist is convinced that the very first forms of life were soft and very perishable, and that therefore no record of them could be preserved in the sedimentary rocks. But the later forms, which led up to and were the parents of those which emerge into view in the Silurian age, must have been capable of fossilization. A record of them doubtless exists somewhere, and may, in time, be brought to light. Darwin thought the record was probably in the rocks beneath the sea, as it is certain the sea and the land have changed places. Or the record may be in the Arctic regions, where some naturalists believe life first began, seeing this part of the earth's surface would be the first to cool and become of a temperature that admitted of animal life. In any case, but a mere fraction of the record — hardly more than a few pages out of many large volumes — is accessible and has been subject to scrutiny. The roots and trunk of our tree must be assumed to have existed. We assume that language began in rude sounds and grunts and signs, as we see it begin in a child, though of course no record of them could be preserved, and that it has developed from these into the marvelous structure which we now behold, branching and refining and specializing almost endlessly.

In the Silurian age, then, we strike the top of our tree of life. All the great branches are represented, all the important classes of animals have made their appearance, even the vertebrates being represented in the upper Silurian by fishes. Of this tree the sub-kingdoms represent the great branches, the classes represent their division, the orders theirs, the family theirs, and so up to species, which represent the terminal twigs. The abundance of specialized forms in the Silurian age, that is, the many smaller branches that appear, and the absence of two generalized forms, or main branches, that must have preceded them, is one of the main obstacles in the way of the evolution theory, a theory of generic descent; but those parent branches, as I have said, are hidden, the record of them has not been found, probably never can be found.

It is very certain, not only from direct evidence, but in the light of analogy, that the forces of nature, vital and other, were much more active in the early geologic ages than they are now. It was the youth of the world; why should they not be more active? Why should there not have been more fluids and gases and more rapid growths and changes? There was more heat, doubtless more rapid evaporation, and more copious precipitation. Our rivers and lakes and water-courses are but a fraction of what they were in comparatively recent geologic times. This tree of life grew rapidly in those warm, moist May and June days of the Silurian and Devonian epochs. New species appeared with comparative suddenness; the life of the globe was full and riotous. Enormous forms began to appear, — flying dragons and terrible and grotesque monsters of the deep. There was a plethora of power, an excess of mere animal life.

But as the ages rolled on, Nature began to sober down: her pace became slower and more deliberate, and she began to rise on stepping-stones of her dead self. The higher forms of life began to appear. Birds emerged, mammals came forth. In the Tertiary age the brains of mammals, according to Marsh, began to increase in size; henceforth the struggle was not to be one of physical strength merely, but intelligence also began to play a part. The maturity of the tree of life was approaching.

That the geological changes were more rapid in the earlier history of the earth than they are now, seems to me to admit of no doubt. The forces of the globe were more restless and titanic. They had not yet attained to the equilibrium and the repose that we now see. The crust of the earth was thinner; the internal fires were nearer; the solid ground was less solid than that we now walk upon.

Volcanoes were more active, earthquakes more frequent. The crust of the earth still throbs and palpitates under the influence of lunar and solar attraction and of unequal atmospheric pressure. Think, then, how much more it must have done so, say in the Silurian age. The cataclysmal theories of the earlier geologists have been much modified by Lyell and his school, but, so far as they imply greater volume and activity in past ages of the physical forces that have shaped the earth, they are doubtless true. In the Tertiary age these forces became much more gentle and uniform in their workings. As changes in the earth's surface would be the most powerful factor in bringing about changes of species, we see why new species seem to have made their appearance so suddenly in early geologic times.

There can be but little doubt that the earth has at last reached the maturity of her powers. She is like a ripe apple upon the bough. Henceforth its excellence must slowly decline. The game of life upon this planet has been essentially played. That is, no new developments remain, no new species on any extended scale, as in the past, are to appear. The bird has been evolved from the reptile, but the bird is doubtless the top of that branch of our tree of life ; no new form is to be evolved from the bird. We know pretty well the evolution of the horse ; he has arisen through various lower and lesser forms, but probably nothing is to come after the horse. The same with other forms. No higher form is to succeed man, as he has succeeded the lower. Monkeys and ourangs are left behind; they will not give birth to a being superior to themselves; they are twigs that have been outstripped by other and more favored branches. Man is the last of the series. Superior races may arise, but not a new and superior type of being. And it is very doubtful about the superior race; there are those who believe the race culminated in the Greeks over two thousand years ago. After the earth has been thoroughly subdued and possessed by the dominant races, as it will be in a few hundred years more, this topmost branch of the tree will probably begin to fail in vitality and fruitfulness. But just what form the decline will take can be only a matter of speculation. We only know that all things have their periods, and are safe in inferring that the life of the globe as a whole will have its period, just as surely as any tree in the forest or any plant in the fields has its period. Why should it not be so? We know any and every single form perishes; why should not the earth itself grow old and die? The life of a man is typical of the life of the earth. The stages of an orb's life, say the astronomers, are stages of cooling. So are the stages of man's life. It is a process of cooling and hardening from youth to age. Think of the gaseous, nebulous youth out

of which the man is gathered and consolidated!
Fiery, stormy, vapory, at first, then cold, hard, ster-
ile at last.

II

DR. JOHNSON AND CARLYLE

GLANCING at a remark in the London "Times,"
the author of "Obiter Dicta," in his late essay on
Dr. Johnson, asks: "Is it as plain as the 'old hill
of Howth' that Carlyle was a greater man than
Johnson? Is not the precise contrary the truth?"
There are very many people, I imagine, who would
be slow to admit that the "precise contrary" was
the truth; yet it is a question not to be decided
offhand. Both were great *men*, unquestionably,
apart from their mere literary and scholastic accomplishments. Each made a profound impression by
virtue of his force of character, his weight and
authority as a person. As to which was the greater
moral, or literary, or political force, as embodied
in his works, it seems to me there can be but one
opinion. But the quantity of manhood each gave
evidence of in his life, and the quantity of genius
he gave evidence of in his books, — these of course
are two different questions. As regards the genius,
Carlyle ranks far above Johnson.

Indeed, the intellectual equipment of the two
men, and the value of their contributions to litera-

ture, admit of hardly any comparison. But the question still is of the man, not of the writer. Which was the greater and more helpful force as a human being? which bore himself the more nobly and victoriously through life? — in short, which was the greater man? Mr. Birrell seems to base his conviction that Johnson was the greater upon the latter's simple resignation and acceptance of the ills of life: —

"Johnson was a man of strong passions, unbending spirit, violent temper; as poor as a church mouse and as proud as the proudest of church dignitaries; endowed with the strength of a coal-heaver, the courage of a lion, and the tongue of Dean Swift, he could knock down booksellers and silence bargees; he was melancholy almost to madness, 'radically wretched,' indolent, blinded, diseased. Poverty was long his portion; not that genteel poverty that is sometimes behindhand with its rent, but that hungry poverty that does not know where to look for its dinner. Against all these things had this 'old struggler' to contend; over all these things did this 'old struggler' prevail. Over even the fear of death, the giving up of this 'intellectual being,' which had haunted his gloomy fancy for a lifetime, he seems finally to have prevailed, and to have met his end as a brave man should."

This is excellently said, and is true enough.

This kind of victory is one test of character certainly; but if it is the highest test by which to try a man's claims to greatness, then is the world full of silent heroes greater than either Johnson or Carlyle. How many men and women receive an avalanche of the ills of life upon their heads and shoulders, and die and make no sign! How many nameless "old strugglers" there are in nearly every community, who fight a losing battle with fortune all their lives and utter no complaint! And it is not always, or commonly, because they are made of pure adamant: it is oftener because they are stolid and insensible. If stolidity and insensibility are terms too strong to apply to Johnson, yet we must admit there was a kind of dullness and sluggishness about him, which he in vain spurred with good resolutions, and which shielded him from the acute suffering that Carlyle's almost preternatural activity and sensibility laid him open to. If a man is born constitutionally unhappy, as both these men seem to have been, his suffering will be in proportion to the strength and vividness of the imagination; and Carlyle's imagination, compared with Johnson's, was like an Arctic night with its streaming and flashing auroras, compared with the midnight skies of Fleet Street.

Carlyle fought a Giant Despair all his life, and never for a moment gave an inch of ground. Indeed, so far as the upshot of his life was concerned, the amount of work actually done, and its value as a tonic and a spur to noble endeavor of all kinds, it is as if he had fought no Giant Despair at all, but had been animated and sustained by the most bright and buoyant hopes. The reason of this probably is that his gloom and despair did not end in mere negation. If he fulminated an Everlasting No, he also fulminated an Everlasting Yes. Johnson fought many lesser devils, such as moroseness, laziness, irritability of temper, gloominess, and tendency to superstition, etc. "My reigning sin," he says in his journal, "to which perhaps many others are appendant, is a waste of time and general sluggishness to which I was always inclined, and, in part of my life, have been almost compelled by morbid melancholy and disturbance of mind. Melancholy has had in me its paroxysms and remissions, but I have not improved the intervals, nor sufficiently resisted my natural inclination, or sickly habits." He was always resolving to rise at eight o'clock in the morning, but does not seem ever to have been able to keep the resolution. What takes one in Johnson is his serious self-reproof and the perfect good faith in which he accuses himself of idleness, forbidden thoughts, a liking for strong liquors, a shirking of church-going, and kindred sins. His sense of duty, and in particular of *his* duty, never slumbered for a moment. On the 21st of April, 1764, he got up at three in the morning to accuse himself thus : "My indolence since my last reception of the Sacrament has sunk into grosser sluggishness, and my dissipation spread into wider negligence. My thoughts have been clouded with sensuality, and, except that from the beginning of this year I have in some measure forborne excess of strong drink, my appetites have predominated over my reason. A kind of strange oblivion has overspread me, so that I know not what has become of the last year," etc. This earthiness, these frailties of Johnson through which his pious hopes and resolutions shine so clearly, is a touch of nature which makes him kin to all the world. Carlyle does not touch us in just this way, because his ills are more imaginary and his language more exaggerated. What takes one in Carlyle is the courage and helpfulness that underlie his despair, the humility that underlies his arrogance, the love and sympathy that lie back of his violent objurgations and in a way prompt them. He was a man of sorrow, and felt the "burthen and the mystery of all this unintelligible world" as Johnson never felt it, nor ever could feel it.

Again, Johnson owed much more to his times than Carlyle did to his. Both his religion and his politics were the religion and the politics of his age and country, and they were like ready-made highways along which his mind and soul traveled. In comparison, Carlyle was adrift in the wilderness, where the way and the bridges had to be built by himself. What gulfs he encountered, what quagmires he floundered through! Johnson "stood by the old formulas," says Carlyle; and adds significantly, "the happier was it for him that he could so stand." What would the great hulking hypochondriac have done in such a world as Carlyle traversed, the ground cut clean from under him by German thought and modern science, awful depths opening where before was solid earth?

Johnson has survived his works. Mr. Birrell declares very emphatically that they are still alive, and are likely to remain so; but the specimens he gives, whether of prose or of verse, are not at all reassuring. But our interest in the man seems likely to be perennial. This is probably because he was a much greater and more picturesque force personally than he was intellectually. His power was of a kind that could not fully be brought to bear in literature, that is to say, he is greater as a talker in personal encounter than in his writings, or in the depth of his thought. He said that "no man but a blockhead ever wrote except for money." But the man who writes for money alone, it is pretty sure, will not make a deep and lasting impression with his pen. The saying is like another one of his, — namely, that "a man seldom thinks with more earnestness of anything than he does of his dinner." When Johnson wrote his famous letter to Lord Chesterfield, it is safe to say he did not write for money, and that he was thinking of something more earnestly than he was wont to think of his dinner; and it is the one piece of his prose that is likely to live. But these remarks of his, and others like them, — this, for instance, that "great abilities are not requisite for an historian; for in historical composition all the greatest powers of the human mind are quiescent," — such remarks, I say, of themselves show his limitations in the direction of literature. Johnson lives through Boswell; without Boswell his fame would hardly have reached our time, except as a faint tradition. In the pages of his biographer the actual man lives for us; we can almost see his great chest heave, and hear the terrible "Sir!" with which he held his interlocutor at good striking distance. If some Boswell had done the same thing for Coleridge, is it probable that he would have lived in the same way? I think not. As a personality, Coleridge was much less striking and impressive than Johnson. As an intellectual force, he is, of course, much more so. But it is hardly possible to feel a deep interest in or admiration for him on personal grounds alone.

Is it possible to feel as deep an interest in and admiration for Carlyle, apart from his works, as we do in Johnson? Different temperaments will answer differently. Some people have a natural antipathy to Carlyle, based largely, no doubt, on misconception. But misconception is much easier in his case than in Johnson's. He was more of an exceptional being. He was pitched in too high a key for the ordinary uses of life. He had fewer infirmities than Johnson, moral and physical. Johnson was a typical Englishman, and appeals to us by all the virtues and faults of his race. Carlyle stood more isolated, and held himself much more aloof from the world. On this account, among others, he touches us less nearly. Women are almost invariably repelled by Carlyle; they instinctively flee from a certain hard, barren masculinity in him. If not a woman-hater, he certainly had little in his composition that responded to the charms and allurements peculiar to the opposite sex; while Johnson's idea of happiness was to spend his life driving briskly in a postchaise with a pretty and intelligent woman. Both men had the same proud independence, the same fearless gift of speech, the same deference to authority or love of obedience. In personal presence, the Englishman had the advantage of mere physical size, breadth, and a stern, forbidding countenance. Johnson's power was undoubtedly more of the chest, the stomach, and less of the soul, than Carlyle's, and was more of a blind, groping, unconscious force; but of the two men he seems the more innocent and childlike. His journal is far less interesting and valuable as literature than Carlyle's; but in some way his fervent prayers, his repeated resolutions to do better, to conquer his laziness, "to consult the resolve on Tetty's coffin," "to go to church," "to drink less strong liquors," "to get up at eight o'clock," "to reject or expel sensual images and idle thoughts," "to read the Scriptures," touch one more nearly than Carlyle's exaggerated self-reproaches and loud bemoanings of the miseries of life. Yet the fact remains that Johnson lived and moved and thought on a lower plane than Carlyle, and that he cherished less lofty ideals of life and of duty. It is probably true, also, that his presence and his conversation made less impression on his contemporaries than did Carlyle's; but, through the wonderful Boswell, a livelier, more lovable, and more real image of him is likely to go down to succeeding ages than of the great Scotchman through his biographer.

III

LITTLE SPOONS *VS.* BIG SPOONS

When I was in England, whether in lodgings or in a hotel, one of the hardest things to get at table was a teaspoon to eat my dessert or sweetmeats with. They always brought a dessert spoon, which usually seems large and awkward to the American mouth. Neither were there any small dishes, such as we have at home. They brought you jam, or preserves, or strawberries, on a plate as large as a dinner plate. This fact would not be worth mentioning, were it not characteristic of much one sees there. In England, nearly all the arts and appliances of life show, to American eyes, a superabundance of material. There is more timber and iron in the wagon, more bulk in the horse that draws the wagon, and more leather in the harness the horse wears. Yes, and more hair in the horse's coat. Our domestic animals, our tools, our vehicles, our architecture, and our women look trim and slim compared with the English. There is probably material enough in an English van to make two of our farm wagons. It is a sight to behold. It looks like a pontoon boat mounted upon huge artillery wheels. It is usually drawn by three horses tandem, with a boy walking by their side or riding the foremost. It would be quite useless in this country, as on our poorly made dirt roads it would be a load in itself. The running works of the English dog-cart, a pleasure vehicle, would be considered nearly heavy enough for a light farm-cart in this country. Easy roads and heavy vehicles are the rule in England, and poor roads and light vehicles with us. John Bull would hardly trust himself in our cobweb "buggies;" certainly not upon our outlandish roads. He does not know the virtues of hickory, a tree native to this country. Hickory gives us the most strength with the least bulk, and this is no doubt one reason of the lightness and slenderness of our tools and vehicles. Compare an English axe with an American axe: how crude and awkward the former looks beside the latter; how shapely our tool is! Our tools suggest a more deft and supple and a lighter race. The tendency in us to pare down and cut away every superfluous ounce is very marked. We are great whittlers. Have we not whittled away at the hulls of our ships until we have made the swiftest sailing vessels in the world?

The English, in most things, seem to like the look of mass and strength; we like best the look of lightness and speed. Even the type in which their books, newspapers, and magazines are printed is larger than the type in which ours are printed. Indeed, it would seem as if there was not room enough in our great country for generous-sized type. English houses and other buildings all have a look of greater solidity than ours; their walls are thicker, their tiles heavier. What would they think of our balloon frames over there? What would our grandfathers think of them? Dickens said the houses in this country looked as if made of pasteboard.

This lightness and airiness is becoming a fixed national trait, and is in keeping with the general tendency of all natural forms in this country. Nearly all organic growths here show greater refine-

ment of form than in the British Isles. Our wild
flowers are more graceful and delicate. Our climbing plants, the foliage of our trees, the trees themselves, our grasses and wild weedy growths, are all
more slender and fluent in form than the corresponding English species. English trees, English groves,
have a wonderful expression of solidity and repose.
The leaves are larger and stiffer, and adjust themselves with more ease to the fainter light. Even
the British bumblebee is a coarser and more hairy
creature than ours ; and the fox and the squirrel,
as well as the domestic animals, are less sleek and
trim than with us. Our bright, sharp climate has
its effect upon all things, but it is only up to a
certain point that this effect is matter for congratulation. All European forms are refined here, but
presently there is danger that they may become
attenuated and weakened. The children of European parents born here — Irish, English, German
— are, as a rule, much more shapely and clear-cut
in feature than when born in the same rank of
life in Europe. But they are less robust and virile,
especially the girls; while, probably, the next generation will be still less so. Here comes in the
setback. What appears to be the most serious danger now threatening the American race is just this
tendency to over-refinement, and the consequent
failure in reproduction.

This tendency has set its stamp upon our mentality, so that our literary and scientific works, and all the varied outcomes of our mental life, are characterized by clearness, quickness, aptness, rather than by force, or depth, or real mastery. Our literature, as such, has less bulk than the English or German, less body and more grace and refinement. Compare Emerson with Carlyle, or Fiske with Spencer, or Hawthorne with Scott, or Prescott with Macaulay, or Howells with George Eliot. Up to a certain point this deftness and clearness of our authors gives them the advantage; but when great tasks are to be undertaken, our lightness and brightness are less telling. Our second considerable crop of authors, born (say) since 1825, has less force, less body, less breadth, than our first great crop, which included Cooper, Bryant, Irving, Emerson, Longfellow, Whittier, etc. There are things in Stedman that have the old breadth and generosity, but there are not enough of them. It seems to me that we are refining now at the expense of strength. Our poets and critics, like our "buggies" and pleasure vehicles, lack timber, lack mass. Our popular novelists have point but lack body. The workmanship is admirable, but the material upon which it is expended is abominable. What a boon to them would be a little of Scott's or Dickens's power and heartiness, or of Turgenieff's grasp of the fundamental human qualities! The men and women turned out are by no means the

equal of those one meets daily among all ranks of
the people, except perhaps in the single qualities
of wit and "smartness." The rank, primary,
inarticulate human qualities are suffering decay
among us; there can be little doubt of that. Probably they are suffering — or are threatened with —
the same decay in Europe. A cheap press, much
and hasty reading, rapid communication, tend to
give us surface dominion without corresponding
depth.

Yet, as contrasted with the American, the Englishman reaps great advantage in his greater stolidity, inertia, mass, depth of character, because
these things make a solid ground to build upon;
and when faculty and insight are added, they give
that weight and force which have made the English
race what it is. There is one notable exception in
our later literature to this American tendency to
over-refinement of form, which I am not likely to
forget; and that is furnished by Walt Whitman.
Mass and strength, and all the primary qualities of
both body and mind, are fully attended to by him.
Probably this, more than anything else, is the reason why his poems are so distasteful to the majority
of his countrymen, and why his reception abroad
has been more cordial than at home. It is, at any
rate, the ground upon which his appearance in our
literature has always been regarded by myself as so
suggestive and so welcome.

BRIEF ESSAYS

IV

THE ETHICS OF WAR

WHY is it that we look so much more complacently upon war, upon a fight between two nations, than we do upon a fight between two individuals? If my neighbor and I have a difficulty or a misunderstanding and proceed to settle it with clubs, or pistols, or with our fists, in the opinion of all decent people we behave shamefully, wickedly, and reduce ourselves to a level with the brutes. But when nations settle their difficulties by an appeal to arms, and thousands upon thousands of lives are sacrificed, and millions upon millions of treasure squandered, we take quite a different view of the matter. We may say, "What a pity!" or "How unwise!" but we do not experience the same feeling of contempt and disgust that we do in the case of personal encounters brought about by like provocation. If two men of rival trades or interests came into collision, and the victor robbed the other of his purse to indemnify himself for his scratches and bruises and torn clothes, he would at once forfeit any sympathy and respect which the justness of his cause might have inspired in the spectators. Instead of a hero we should look upon him as a robber. Yet Germany beats France in battle, and indemnifies herself for her bruises and torn clothes by a large slice of French territory and many millions of French treasure, and we do not feel that she has sacrificed her honor. Does might make right between nations, while the principle will not hold good at all as between individuals?

It is certainly true that we do not apply the same standard of morality in the one case that we do in the other, — certainly true that we do not look for the same acts of generosity or magnanimity between nations that we expect to be shown between neighbors. Nations are invariably selfish, and they are rarely as honest as their individual citizens. Legislative bodies have deliberately done things, or refrained from doing things, that the individual members composing them would blush to be found guilty of. What meanness, narrowness, selfishness, has not England been guilty of? and yet the individual Englishman is by no means insensible to the obligations of truth and fair play. States and communities in this country have repudiated their honest debts in a way that would have ruined the standing of any business man in them had he resorted to the same trick to defraud his creditors. The American Congress had for more than fifty years behaved in the most shameful and dishonest manner in refusing to authorize the payment of the French spoliation claims. The precepts of religion have had little or no influence upon the policy of nations. Love your neighbor as yourself; do unto others as you would that others should do unto you; think no evil, — what should we think if governments acted upon these principles? Is the nation, then, a remnant of barbarism that the moral law should not apply to it? that religion should not affect it?

It is because nations are not as civilized as individuals, and, probably, never will be, that war is still possible. The nation is still the tribe, and the tribal instincts for self-preservation are still active; tribal jealousies and animosities are still easily kindled. Our admiration for war is the same as our admiration for the virtues of the stern heroic ages, — courage, self-sacrifice, contempt of death, personal prowess, great leadership. The nation, as such, still rests upon these qualities. Genius and power always take us, and war is a great field for the display of genius and power.

All readers of "Sartor Resartus" will remember the striking, though not quite just, light in which Carlyle sets war: —

"What, speaking in quite unofficial language, is the net purpose and upshot of war? To my own knowledge, for example, there dwell and toil in the British village of Dumdrudge usually some five hundred souls. From these, by certain natural enemies of the French, there are successively selected during the French war, say thirty able-bodied men. Dumdrudge, at her own expense, has suckled and nursed them; she has, not without difficulty and sorrow, fed them up to manhood, and even trained them to crafts, so that one can weave, another build, another hammer, and the weakest can stand under thirty stone avoirdupois. Nevertheless, amid much weeping and swearing, they are selected; all dressed in red, and shipped away on the public charges some two thousand miles, or say only to the south of Spain; and fed there till wanted. And now to that same spot in the south of Spain are thirty similar French artisans, from a French Dumdrudge, in like manner wending; till at length, after infinite effort, the two parties come into actual juxtaposition; and thirty stands fronting thirty, each with a gun in his hand. Straightway the word 'Fire!' is given; and they blow the souls out of one another; and in place of sixty brisk, useful craftsmen, the world has sixty dead carcasses which it must bury and anew shed tears for. Had these men any quarrel? Busy as the devil is, not the smallest! They lived far enough apart; were the entirest strangers; nay, in so wide a universe, there was even, unconsciously, by Commerce, some mutual helpfulness between them. How then? Simpleton! their Governors had fallen out; and instead of shooting one another, had the cunning to make these poor blockheads shoot."

This is very witty, but is it a true picture of modern war? The Governors of these sixty men had not fallen out; they had no personal quarrel; they may even have had a warm feeling of friendship for each other; it was in their representative capacities that they had a quarrel; the two nations quarreled through them, and it is fit the two nations should send men to fight it out, and that the Governors themselves should keep out of harm's way. It is the narrow feeling of patriotism, of sectionalism, and race prejudices that make wars possible. The European nations are jealous and suspicious of each other, like African tribes. Did they all form one federation, and see that the best interests of one were in the end the best interests of all, war between them would be impossible.

Our admiration for war, then, is a mixed feeling, in some of its elements laudable, in others questionable. Our love of the heroic overrides our humanitarian feelings; our attraction for power blunts our sense of right. If a man steals a chicken, we hold him in contempt, but if he steals a railroad, we feel quite differently toward him. Anybody can rob a henroost, but it requires a genius and capacity to steal a great corporate interest. But there are grounds upon which our admiration for war is laudable. In the first place, war is not personal, as a quarrel between individuals is; the personal feelings of anger, hatred, etc., which brutalize men in personal conflicts, are not appealed to. It is a school of discipline in all the more manly and heroic virtues. It begets courage, coolness, self-control. It is a great game between great forces, in which the

231

clearest and longest heads win. It fosters patriotism and the feeling of nationality. It is said of certain African tribes that those that are the most warlike as nations are the least so as individuals, and *vice versa*. Quarrelsome and vindictive men do not make good soldiers. The most peaceable and high-minded make the best. The more brutal qualities that seek personal encounter are not the qualities that inspire a great soldiery. It is not an encounter between men wherein one seeks in a passion of anger to overthrow the other and aggrandize himself; it is a collision of the great forces that rule men. Moral force does as much, or more, than physical force. The great passion or inspiration of heroism has play; men are called upon to face great odds; they are called upon to offer their lives for others. Men who lead a charge and do not flinch or turn back have achieved the noblest victory over themselves, whether they break the enemy or not. The element of destiny comes in. Large bodies of men are subject to laws and conditions that touch not the individual. Their wrath is not as the wrath of a man; their blood-shedding is not as the crime of a person. So many elements enter into a great battle beside the personal element; all the forces of nature take part. It often happened in the ancient wars that the army was defeated that had the sun in its eyes. Often some false rumor, some accidental cry, turns the tide.

The *morale* of an army is everything: faith in their general and in the justness of their cause, — there are no reinforcements like these. Indeed, every impulse that is manly and noble and elevating tells tremendously in war.

These are perhaps some of the considerations that lead us to judge war between nations by a different standard from the one we apply to individual encounters. It has not the demoralizing element of base anger. There must be something that vastly more than offsets the brutal element in it, else the good could never have flowed from it that we know has flowed. Men who settle their differences by blows and blood are always the worse for it. But nations are often the better for it. It sets new and larger currents going. The nation is above the individual, and the national life is often cemented and strengthened by the blood of the best citizens.

V

SOLITUDE

EMERSON says, "Now and then a man exquisitely made can live alone, and must; but coop up most men and you undo them." Solitude tries a man in a way society does not; it throws him upon his own resources, and if these resources be meagre, if the ground he occupies in and of himself be poor and narrow, he will have a sorry time of it. Hence we readily attribute some extra virtue to those persons who voluntarily embrace solitude, who live alone in the country or in the woods, or in the mountains, and find life sweet. We know they cannot live without converse, without society of some sort, and we credit them with the power of invoking it from themselves, or else of finding more companionship with dumb things than ordinary mortals. In any case they give evidence of resources which all do not possess. If not "exquisitely made," hermits generally have a fine streak in them, which preserves them in solitude. If a man wants to get away from himself, or from a guilty conscience, he does not retreat into the country, he flees to the town. If he is empty, the town will fill him; if he is idle, the town will amuse him; if he is vain, here is a field for his vanity; if he is ambitious, here are dupes waiting to be played upon; but if he is an honest man, here he will have a struggle to preserve his integrity. The rapid growth of cities in our time has its dark side. Every man who has a demon to flee from, a vice to indulge, an itching for notoriety to allay, money to squander, or a dream of sudden wealth to cherish, flees to the city, and, as most persons have one or the other of these things, the city outstrips the country. It is thought that the more a man is civilized, the more his tastes are refined, the more he will crave city life and the more benefit he will get from it. But this may be questioned. It is not, as a rule, a refined taste that takes men to cities, but a craving for a vain superficial elegance, the pride of dress, of equipage, of fashion, of fast living, and the shams and follies of the world. The more simple and refined taste loves the seriousness and sobriety of the country.

People find country life dull because they are empty and frivolous; having only themselves on their hands, they can extract no entertainment from such a subject. How can a man profitably commune with himself, if the self is small and frivolous and unworthy? He will not go to his own garden for fruit if there be only thorns there.

The finest spirits are not gregarious; they do not love a crowd. Crows and wolves go in flocks and packs, but the eagle and the lion are solitary in their habits.

Solitude is not for the young; the young have no thoughts or experiences, but only unsatisfied desires; it is for the middle-aged and the old, for a man when he has ripened and wants time to mellow his thoughts. A man who retires into solitude must have a capital of thought and experience to live upon, or his soul will perish of want. This capital must be reinvested in the things about him, or it will not suffice. Either as a farmer or as a student and lover of nature, or as both, can he live

as it were on the interest of his stored-up wisdom.

"There are things that never show themselves
till you are alone," said an old recluse in Mexico
to an American traveler who had claimed the hos-
pitality of his hut; "but if you once make up your
mind that there is no harm in them, you find out
that they are pretty good company." The old recluse knew what he was saying. Things do show
themselves when one is alone; they emerge on all
sides; they come in troops from all points of the
compass, and one is only master of the situation
when he can make good company of them. How
your misdeeds find you out! the still small voice of
conscience, which you could not hear amid the roar
of the town, makes itself heard now; all the past
beleaguers you, — whether with an army of angels
or of demons, depends upon what your past has
been.

The old recluse above referred to, the traveler
found living in a hut alone in the mountains. He
had lived there many years, with no companionship
but his dogs. An Irishman by birth, he had tried
many parts of the world, and seen many phases of
life, and had at last found his place in the solitude
of the Mexican mountains. He had learned the art
of dreaming with his eyes open, which is the charm
of solitude. A man who cannot dream with his eyes
open had better not court solitude. Such an old

dreamer was found the other day by some rail-road surveyors on a mountain in North Carolina. He had lived there in his hut for fifty years. He, too, had for companion a dog. If Thoreau had made friends with a dog to share his bed and board in his retreat by Walden Pond, one would have had more faith in his sincerity. The dog would have been the seal and authentication of his retreat. A man who has no heart for a dog, — how can he have a heart for Nature herself? For many reasons women seldom voluntarily face solitude, but in my boyhood I knew an aged widow who lived all alone on her little farm, in her little brown house, for many years. She kept five or six cows, which she took care of herself, winter and summer. She hired her hay gathered, her wood cut, and that was all. She was a gentle and pious little woman, and her house was as neat as a pin. But think of those long years of solitary life; the nights, the mornings, the meals, the Sundays, the week days, and no sound but what you made yourself! How intimately acquainted with one's self one must become in such a life! If one's self was not a pretty good fellow, how cordially one would learn to dislike his company! One Sunday, as my people were passing the house on their way to church, they saw her washing. "Hello, Aunt Debby! don't you know it is Sunday?" Behold the consternation of the old dame! She had lost her reckoning, and had kept Sabbath on Saturday. The last time I passed that way I saw only a little grassy mound where Aunt Debby's house used to stand.

The poet of solitude is Wordsworth. What a sense of the privacy of fields and woods there is over all his poetry; what stillness, what lonesome dells, what sounds of distant waterfalls! How fondly he lingers upon the simple objects of nature, upon rural scenes and events, and how perpetually he returns upon his own heart! His companionship with hills and trees and rocks and shepherds does not relieve, but rather sets off, his loneliness. He is encompassed with solitude wherever he goes:—

> "In November days,
> When vapors rolling down the valley make
> A lonely scene more lonesome; among woods
> At noon; and mid the calm of summer nights,
> When by the margin of the trembling lake,
> Beneath the gloomy hills I homeward went
> In solitude;"

and has the same sweet and fruitful fellowship with nature and with his own heart. In his "A Poet's Epitaph" he has drawn his own portrait:—

> "He is retired as noontide dew,
>   Or fountain in a noonday grove;
> And you must love him, ere to you
>   He will seem worthy of your love.

Evening at Rydal Water

"The outward shows of sky and earth,
    Of hill and valley, he has viewed;
  And impulses of deeper birth
    Have come to him in solitude.

"In common things that round us lie
    Some random truths he can impart, —
  The harvest of a quiet eye
    That broods and sleeps on his own heart."

Wordsworth was solitary because of his profound seriousness, and because great thoughts or deep emotions always create a solitude of their own. What is communing with nature but communing with ourselves? Nature gives back our thoughts and feelings, as we see our faces reflected in a pool. Wordsworth found himself whenever he walked; all nature was Wordsworthian. Another man of equal profundity and sympathy finds nature stamped with his image.

Wordsworth felt akin to all solitary things; he is drawn by every recluse and wanderer; he loves to contemplate beggars, and dwellers or watchers in secluded dells, and to sing the praises of "The Solitary Reaper." A solitary flower, a solitary scene of almost any kind, never failed to move him. What a charm of seclusion in the poem beginning,

"I wandered lonely as a cloud
    That floats on high o'er vales and hills."

Or in this other, —

> "I heard a thousand blended notes
>   While in a grove I sat reclined
>   In that sweet mood where pleasant thoughts
>   Bring sad thoughts to the mind."

Or again in this immortal song, —

> "She dwelt among the untrodden ways,
>   Beside the springs of Dove,
>   A maid whom there were none to praise
>   And very few to love:

> "A violet by a mossy stone
>   Half hidden from the eye;
>   Fair as a star when only one
>   Is shining in the sky."

Before Wordsworth, solitude had a lover and poet in Abraham Cowley. Through nearly all his essays there runs a desire to escape from the world, and to be alone with nature and with his own thoughts. And who has better expressed this desire and the satisfaction which its fulfillment brings? He longed for the country as an exile longs for home. He says to Evelyn that he had never had any other desire so strong and so like to covetousness as the one he had always had, namely, to be master at last of a small house and a large garden, with very moderate conveniences joined to them, and there to dedicate the remainder of his life only to the culture of them and to the study of nature.

He says: "As far as my memory can return back into my past life, before I knew or was capable of guessing what the world or the glories or business of it were, the natural affections of my soul gave me a secret bent of aversion from them." When he was a boy at school, he was wont to leave his playfellows, and walk alone into the fields. How charmingly he praises "Obscurity," and how pungently he sets forth the "Dangers of an honest man in much company!"

He knew well the virtues which solitude necessitated and implied.

"The truth of the matter is, that neither he who is a fop in the world is a fit man to be alone; nor he who has set his heart much upon the world, though he have never so much understanding: so that solitude can be well fitted and sit right but upon a very few persons. They must have enough knowledge of the world to see the vanity of it, and enough virtue to despise all vanity; if the mind be possessed with any lust or passion, a man had better be in a fair than in a wood alone."

But, after all has been said about the solitude of nature, that is the best solitude that comes clothed in the human form, — your friend, your other self, who leaves you alone, yet cheers you; who peoples your house or your field and wood with tender remembrances; who stands between your yearning heart and the great outward void that you try in vain to warm and fill; who in his own person and spirit clothes for you, and endows with tangible form, all the attractions and subtle relations and meanings that draw you to the woods and fields. What the brooks and the trees and the birds said so faintly and vaguely, he speaks with warmth and directness. Indeed, your friend complements and completes your solitude, and you experience its charm without its desolation. I cannot, therefore, agree with Marvell that

> "Two paradises are in one,
>   To live in paradise alone."

I should want at least my friend to share it with me.

VI

AN OPEN DOOR

How the revelations of science do break in upon the sort of private and domestic view of the universe which mankind have so long held! To many minds it is like being fairly turned out into the cold, and made to face without shield or shelter the eternities and the infinities of geologic time and sidereal space. We are no longer cozily housed in pretty little anthropomorphic views of things. The universe is no longer a theatre constructed expressly for the drama of man's life and salvation. The race of man becomes the mere ephemera of an hour, like insects of a summer day. In an hour of the summer of the earth's geologic history he appears, and in an hour he is gone; a few hours more and all is gone, and the earth itself is frozen into the everlasting death and night of the winter of the solar system. Science says in just so many words, "There is no reason to deny the final cessation of the sun's activity, and the consequent death of the system."

Our hearts, our affections, all our peculiarly human attributes, draw back from many of the deductions of science. We feel the cosmic chill. We cannot warm or fill the great void. The universe seems orphaned. This is the reason why many people, who accept science with their understanding, still repudiate it in their hearts; the religious beliefs of their youth still meet a want of their natures.

It makes a great difference whether we look upon things from the point of view of our personal wants and needs, or from the point of view of reason. It takes mankind, as it takes every individual man, a long and hard struggle to break away from the former standpoint, and to gain the mountain-top implied in the latter. When I look upon the sun from my place and surroundings, he seems to be a

mere appurtenance of the earth. How he seems
to attend us, and to swing around us to give light
and warmth ! How immense seems the earth ; how
small, comparatively, the sun! See him setting
behind the hills or riding up out of the wave!
Xenophanes, according to Plutarch, thought the
earth had many suns and many moons. An eclipse
of the sun, he said, happened when the orb of the
sun, falling upon some part of the world which is
uninhabited, wandered in a vacuum and became
eclipsed. Herodotus also looked upon the sun as
something thus special to the earth. On the approach of winter, he says, he grows feeble and
retreats to the south, because he can no longer face
the cold and the storms of the north. One is
reminded of these things when he sees the good
people appropriate God to themselves in a way they
are perpetually doing. What a special interest He
takes in their lives! Their well-being or their ill-
being seems his main concern. All the early races
— the Bible races — do this. How the old He-
brews claimed God ! He was the Lord God of
Israel and of no one else. How imminent, how
personal, He is in their Scriptures; how cruel, how
terrible, how jealous, — a magnified and heaven-
filling despot and king! All the good old pious
people still refer the events of their daily lives to
Providence. Indeed, the popular conception of
God is still essentially Ptolemaic. Our religion is

built upon the notion that man and man's life are the objects of his especial care and solicitude. And so they are, but not just in the way we are so fond of thinking.

Astronomers figure out for us the infinitesimal fraction of the sun's light which our earth intercepts in the infinite void; in the same way and to the same extent does the providence of God transcend not only the wants of our little lives, but the life of the globe itself. Yet each and all get enough. The sun seems near to us, — is near by its power. The light that floods our houses, that shines upon our fields, — how potent it is! What marvelous transformations it works! If the sun did, indeed, shine for this world alone, and was only just there behind the horizon as it seems, we could not be better looked after.

To all intents and purposes, God is and exists for each one of us alone. His providence is exemplified in every movement of our lives. Out of the abuse of this feeling or faith comes our arrogating to ourselves special providences, special interference in our petty affairs. But until the sun does shoot some special ray for you, and the attraction of gravity make some exception in your favor, count not upon God's doing so. Our very life, the beating of our very hearts, depends upon the sun, not because the sun is special, but because the sun is universal; not because it is adjusted and adapted to us, but because we are adjusted and adapted to it. Its bounty and power extend in every direction alike; it shoots into the void myriads of rays as vivifying as those that make our blood flow. The same with this power we call God. In it we live and move and have our being, but it is not an attendant of our lives; we are an accident of it; it is imminent to us, because it is imminent everywhere. Light was not made for the eye, but we have eyes because there is light. The outward world is not accommodated to us, but *vice versa*. There are no special acts of Providence that have reference to you and to me, to this or to that event of our lives, any more than the North Star was placed there for the guidance of mariners, or that anything in nature was made for the use of man. Was water made to quench thirst? No; we have thirst because there is water. Were the beauties and harmonies of nature made to delight our senses or for our edification? No; we have the sense of the beautiful because beauty exists. The beneficent forces of nature brought us forth and sustain us, therefore we love beneficence. The loving-kindness and the tender mercies of God, of which we hear so much, are such not because they are directed to us, but because they are directed to all, — because the laws of the universe are so, and not otherwise. God answers prayer, not by a particular providence, but by a general providence. You may light your fire by focusing the sun's rays with a burning-glass; but the rays are no different; they are the same as those that are shot into space on all sides at all times. Still, Providence is imminent in human affairs, not by special acts, but by universal, eternal, unceasing acts. Does it rain to make things grow and to fill our wells and cisterns? We are apt to take this view of things, but I noticed that it rained at sea the same as upon the land. Men and nations at war with each other, each seeking to slay or overthrow the other, pray to the same God for victory. And God helps one just as much as He helps the other, not by special providences, but by general providences, like the rain or snow, or light or gravitation. His laws prevail, and whoso obeys them (his will) best triumphs; God gives him the victory. I notice that when the children of Israel are defeated, or suffer any disaster, God is always against them; but when they triumph, it is God who gives the victory, and it is all true in a strict scientific sense.

A clergyman on the wrecked train thanked God most fervently that the train did not go into the river. It was clearly the hand of Providence that saved them, he said. One would have thought that if God had interested himself at all in the incident, He would have interested himself to have prevented it. If not, we must either suppose He was unable to prevent it, or else unwilling, and either horn of the dilemma is a bad horn. At New Hamburg, a few years ago, when a passenger train ran into an oil train, and hundreds of people perished, He seems to have taken no hand at all in the matter. Why should He save this crowd and not that? Or the Ashtabula horror, — where was God then? Hiding from the disaster He might have averted? Ah me! as soon as we make God out to be a person who interferes in the events of this world, into what straits are we forced! We are forced to conclude either that He is not omnipotent, or else that He is a monster of cruelty, — that He is capricious and changeable, or an ogre that delights in human suffering and blood. I know the well-known text we take shelter under, — the ways of Providence are past finding out; but that is begging the question. You presume to know them and to have found them out when you say He chose to throw the train on the upper side of the track instead of on the lower. No, He is not that kind of a God. The only way He interferes or takes a hand is through the eternal laws which He has established. In this case the laws of force, the laws of resistance and of matter, were the hand of God that threw the train against the bank; had the forces clashed a little differently, the train would have gone into the river. No miracle was performed to prevent it. A good engineer could tell you exactly how it happened. And yet the feeling to thank God in such a case is a natural one and a worthy one; it proceeds from a true religious attitude of the soul.

The balance, the adjustment, the equipoise which we see in the physical world, and which we see in the world of man, too, was not brought about by any guidance or principle of action that bears the slightest resemblance to human methods and aims, but is the result of eons upon eons of conflict, of clashing, of waste and destruction, the fittest or the luckiest surviving. What principle of benevolence, or of justice, or of wise foresight has regulated the distribution of the various human races upon the globe, or determined the relative ascendency of the various nationalities? Just the principle that determines which of a hungry pack of dogs shall get and keep the bone you toss them. Think of the wrongs, the cruelties, the waste, the slaughters of history. Think of that mad carnival of lust and power which the history of the Roman Empire alone shows. The past of the race is knee-deep with blood, largely innocent blood, and the past of nature is black with convulsion and struggle. Admitted that good has come out of it all, yet how unlike has been the method to anything we know as goodness or benevolence! Good has come out of it because our constitutions are adapted to it. To us it is good; to differently constituted beings it might be bad. The principle or power which underlies all things is like the principle of gravitation, which is exerted equally in all directions, and which spares no crashing or crushing, no floods of water or downfall of mountains, or subsidence of continents, in bringing about the equilibrium which we behold. Some things sink and some things swim; but whichever it be, gravity has its way. There is no waste in nature; waste in nature is but taking out of one pocket and putting into the other.

Prayer is practically a belief in miracles or special providences, — a belief that the world is governed, not by immutable law, but by a being whose favor may be won, whose anger may be appeased, or whose purpose may be changed, like that of a great monarch or king. "Most men, in their prayers," says Turgenieff, "ask God that two and two may not make four." "The best prayers," says Joubert, "are those which have nothing distinct, and which thus partake of adoration. God listens but to thoughts and sentiments." "To ask is to receive, when we ask for a genuine good," because the genuine good is in the devout and sincere asking; but convince your orthodox neighbor of this, and he will probably cease to pray. Prayer with him is a petition to some power external to himself for some definite, tangible, measurable good. He will pray for rain or for sun; and the faith which prompts him is a stay to him, whether the rain comes or not. The wisest man cannot pray, has no need of prayer, because his whole life is an aspiration toward, and a desire for, the supreme good of the world.

In every emergency that requires courage and presence of mind, the great danger is in the fear of danger. The man who, lost in the woods or on the plains, or going into battle, prays earnestly to God for help and guidance, has his wits and senses sharpened and his courage strengthened by that act of faith. Because this is so, because mankind have in all ages, the pagan as well as the Christian, been blessed by sincere prayer to their gods, they have come finally to pervert and vulgarize prayer by asking for outward material good. To pray for rain is like praying for a change in the moon or in the tides and seasons. All Christendom prayed for President Garfield, but without avail, because the wound was mortal. Did prayer ever stop the yellow fever before frost came? Is it ever safe to let your piety offset sanitary observances? If sewer gas gets into your house, will holiness keep the distemper out? No; and vaccination is a better safeguard against smallpox than prayer, however fervent and serious.

What remains, then, for those who cannot pray; who cannot look upon God as a being apart from themselves, a supreme parent, seated somewhere in the universe, and withholding or bestowing gifts and goods upon man? This alone, and this is enough: To love virtue, to love truth, to cherish a lofty ideal, to keep the soul open and hospitable to whatsoever things are true, to whatsoever things are beautiful, to whatsoever things are of good report.

VII

THE TRUE REALISM

WITHOUT at all aiming to impeach the value of what is known in current criticism as realism in art, I think it may safely be said that any imaginative work, or any work aspiring to the rank of literature, which does not afford a sure and a speedy escape into the ideal, is of little value.

The true literary artist is not afraid of the real, the concrete ; indeed, he loves real things as the painter his pigments, but they are only a means to an end, and that end is not the literal truth, but the ideal truth. Strict fidelity to nature, to fact, is to be demanded, and equal fidelity to the spirit, the imagination. The artist must give us a true picture, but he must give us much more than that; he must give us himself.

It is the province of literature to make us free of the ideal, and of science to make us acquainted with demonstrable fact. It seems to me it matters little whether a writer draws his material from what we call the real, or from the ideal, so that the result be good literature. Why exalt the realist at the expense of the idealist? Why commend Zola's method over that of Hawthorne, when both are failures unless they reach and move the imagination, and both succeed when they do move it?

If in such a connection one may be allowed to speak of his own work, I may say that I should think much more meanly of my own books than I do, if I did not believe that my account of bird, or flower, or forest, or stream, contained some stimulus or quality, or suggestion, which the reality itself does not hold, and which is purely the gift of the spirit. Your fact or observation is not literature until it is put in some sort of relation to the soul.

There probably never was a time when the craving for the real in art — the real as opposed to the fantastic, the impossible, or the visionary — was more acute than it is now; but the need and the demand are equally urgent for that real to be set in such a light, or in such relation to the mind, that it fuse readily with the spirit and become one with it. The soul of man is the source and the only source of that charm which a true work of art possesses. The real itself, however faithfully set forth, has no charm. A photograph is barren; the rudest sketch of the same, seen by a true artist, has far more power to touch and move the soul. Only the man who looks upon the real with passion, with emotion, will succeed in transmuting it into something higher, and thus permanently interest mankind in it. And if he looks upon the imaginary, the fantastic, with passion and emotion, he will interest mankind in that also. He will make that real and living to us.

"The highest problem of any art," says Goethe, "is to produce by semblance the illusion of some higher reality. But it is a false endeavor to realize the appearance until at last only something commonly real remains."

I think the complaint one has to make of the current realistic fiction is that it fails to produce this "illusion of some higher reality." It rests with the "commonly" or meanly realistic. After we have finished the book, we feel as if we had been in the company of people whose acquaintance was not worth the making. They are or may be copied from our friends and acquaintances, but there is this difference: In real life, there is something, it may not be easy to say just what, that gives pathos and significance to the most humdrum and frivolous, — something that points to the higher reality; but in the story the people are cut off, isolated, and we feel only their pettiness or silliness. It is often said that the commonest and dullest life, if truly written, would have something of perennial interest; but it must be sympathetically written, and shown off against a proper background. There are few more commonplace characters in themselves in fiction than Partridge in "Tom Jones," but Partridge witnessing his first play at the theatre is immortal. The meanest life has poetry in it, but it takes a poet to bring the poetry out. In writing "Werther," Goethe said he succeeded in breathing into the work "all that warmth which leaves no distinction between the poetical and the actual." Whether or not it was realistic, in the sense that it was a faithful picture of the life of his times, is of little moment compared with the question: Was it vital and serious, or informed with real passion? And if the passion of the story or poem is real, do we care for any other reality? If the mood and temper in which an author contemplates his subject are genuine, his realism will take care of itself.

Paradoxical as it may seem, it is only the idealist who can adequately deal with the real, — who can fuse it and use it and bring out its full significance. There may be a barren realism, just as well as a barren idealism; the proper marriage of the two is the end and aim of art. To make the idea tangible to us, whether in poetry or in prose, so that the mind can rest upon it, and feel braced and excited by it, — is not that also an end to be aimed at? And, on the other hand, to make the actual, the concrete, fluid and plastic, and inform it with meaning and power, — is not that also to be striven for? In the same proportion in which literature is real, must it also be ideal; just so much earth as there is, just so much sky must arch over it. The actual must be transmuted, the ideal must be embodied; both must be brought within the sphere of the spiritual faculty and fixed there. If the novelist transfers to his page the real life about him and adds no charm or illusion or suggestion from his own spirit, he is less a realist than he is a materialist; his work has little value. The writers who can describe the actual and make it real to us, that is, make us share their experience and their emotion, are very rare. They tell us what they saw or what they felt, but they do not put the reader in the presence of the actual thing or occurrence. How many historians make the past alive again for us? Only the man with an enormous grasp of the ideal, or great imaginative power, can do it. Shakespeare can do it, Carlyle can do it. What a sense of reality in all Carlyle's histories! The dead reality is not enough; it must be made alive again. Equally few are the writers who can make the ideal tangible or warm to us.

In any case, whatever the theme, the first requisite in the mind of the writer is a vivid sense of reality. I sometimes think this sense of reality the main thing which distinguishes the master from the tyro. In the great writer, in whatever field, we encounter real things, real values, real differences, real emotions, real impressions; his sense of reality always saves him from phantoms. The mind in which this sense of reality is weak, no matter whether it deals with the concrete or the abstract, will always fail to make an impression.

For my part, I want no better realists than the great masters of the ideal, from Homer down to Hawthorne and Turgenieff. How they all differ both in their material and treatment! but in the page of each you encounter that reality, that sense of substance and vitality, which are to the mind what the ground is to the foot, or the air to the lungs.

VIII

LITERARY FAME

GOLDSMITH, according to Boswell, said that he had come too late into the world; that Pope and other poets had carried off all the literary prizes. Dr. Johnson confirmed the remark, and said it was difficult to get literary fame, and was every day becoming more and more difficult. This is probably the feeling of all writers who have reached the measure of their powers ; they mistake the limits of their own tether for the end of the world. The possibilities that are not open to them they think do not exist. A man of genius and power makes the world his own, and when he is done with it, he fancies there is nothing left. Every one of us repeats the same experience on a different scale. As our careers draw to a close, we fancy we have exhausted the whole of life, and that there will be nothing left for those who are to come after us. But life is always new to the new man. Think of the great names in British literature since Goldsmith and Johnson; think of Burns, Wordsworth, Scott, Byron, Dickens, Macaulay, Carlyle, Arnold, etc., each one of whom, probably, in exhausting his own possibilities fancied he had exhausted the possibilities of nature.

Probably literary fame is no more difficult of achievement at one time than at another, just as easy to Thackeray as it was to Goldsmith; and this notwithstanding that an achievement that would have given a measure of fame a century ago would attract far less attention to-day. Is it at all likely that if the "Spectator" essays were written to-day they would attract any considerable notice, or that the "Idler" and "Adventurer" would find any readers? But the writer of to-day has all this past to stand upon, he profits by all these accumulated achievements. A man is largely the creature of his times; he is strong by the strength of the age in which he lives. An invention that would have seemed marvelous a century ago might be a very tame affair to-day; and yet the same genius, the same power in achieving a noteworthy result to-day, would probably have no more obstacles to overcome, or mysteries to solve, than one hundred years ago. He has a great fund to work with; he sees farther because he stands higher. If the achievement is measured by the standard of to-day, it is to be remembered that the achiever is strong by the strength of to-day. The same in science. Now the quarry is so thoroughly opened, larger and more valuable results ought to be easier than ever before. Of course the poet or literary man cannot avail himself of the results of the labor of others in the same way the man of science can and does, but he cannot escape the general lift of the age in which he lives; he shares in the momentum, moral and intellectual, of his contemporaries. In a certain sense, also, he inherits, as an available personal fund, what others have done before him. It is the common mind which has been refined and enlarged, and of this advantage he partakes. Literature is an investment of genius which pays dividends to all subsequent times.

If nature were guilty of endless repetition in turning out men of exceptional powers, of course every new man would find his task already done in the world; but nature forever varies the pattern so that the new man has a new standpoint and sees things in new combinations and discovers new values, and he is never forestalled by those who have gone before him. Every new genius is an impossibility until he appears; we cannot forecast his type. He is a revelation, and through his eyes we shall see undreamed-of effects. It is doubtful if contemporary writers of original power ever stand in each other's way. There is always room and demand for any number of original men. The lesser poets of course suffer in competition with the greater; the large stars draw our eyes away from the smaller; we should make more of Bayard Taylor, for instance, if he were our only poet; but is it probable that Longfellow or Whittier or Bryant or Emerson ever intercepted any portion of the fame due and within reach of the other? Have Tennyson or Browning in any sense ever been rivals? Literary fame is not a limited quantity which must lessen in proportion as it is divided up, but, like the sunlight, each man may have it all and not rob his neighbor. Inventors and discoverers and men of science may anticipate each other, but literary genius can never be anticipated; the value of the gift which it brings is in its uniqueness. I heard it remarked the other day of one of our promising young poets that his work lacked flavor. It is this flavor which is indispensable, and which can never be forestalled by another. There is rivalry in the trades and the professions, but you poet, or you novelist, or you essayist, if your work has flavor or character of its own, your chance for fame is just as good as if there were no competitors in the field. It is not a vacant niche in the Temple of Fame which you are striving for, and which only one can fill: it is a niche in the hearts of men, where the room is boundless.

Goldsmith felt himself under the shadow of Pope's great fame, but of course he was a gainer from Pope's career. His performance was as unique as Pope's, and has probably been of more service to mankind. But Pope cleared and sharpened the mind of his age; dull wits found less acceptance after than before him, and in this benefit Goldsmith, like others, was a sharer.

IX

AN EGOTISTICAL CHAPTER

A FEW years ago the editor of a popular magazine inveigled a good many people, myself among the number, into writing about themselves and their experiences in life. None of us, I imagine, needed very much persuading, for as a rule there is no subject which a man or a woman is more ready or willing to talk about than himself or herself. One's ailments are always a favorite subject; next to that, one's good luck or ill luck in his last undertaking; then one's experiences, one's likes and dislikes; and lastly, self-analysis and criticism. And it has been said that a man "is never so sure to please as when he writes of himself with good faith, and without affectation." Ay, there's the rub ; to write of one's self without affectation! A false note of this kind is fatal to the interest and value of the criticism.

In a certain sense, a man of the literary or artistic temperament never portrays or writes of anything but himself ; that is, he gives us things as seen through the intimate personal medium which he himself is. All things reflect his hue and quality.

This is the bane of science, but it is the life of literature. I have probably unwittingly written myself in my books more fully and frankly than I ever can by any direct confession and criticism; but the latter may throw some side light at least, and, on looking over what I wrote for the editor above referred to, I find that portions of it possess a certain interest and value to myself, and therefore I trust may not seem entirely amiss to my reader.

If a man is not born into the environment best suited to him, he, as a rule, casts about him until he finds such environment. My own surroundings and connections have been mainly of the unliterary kind. I was born of and among people who neither read books nor cared for them, and my closest associations since have been with those whose minds have been alien to literature and art. My unliterary environment has doubtless been best suited to me. Probably what little freshness and primal sweetness my books contain is owing to this circumstance. Constant intercourse with bookish men and literary circles I think would have dwarfed or killed my literary faculty. This perpetual rubbing of heads together, as in the literary clubs, seems to result in literary sterility. In my own case, at least, what I most needed was what I had, — a few books and plenty of real things. I never had any aptitude for scholarly attainments; my verbal or artificial memory, so to speak, was poor, but my mind always had a certain magnetic or adhesive quality for things that were proper to it and that belonged to me.

I early took pleasure in trying to express myself on paper, probably in my sixteenth or seventeenth year. In my reading I was attracted by everything of the essay kind. In the libraries and bookstores I was on the lookout for books of essays. And I wanted the essay to start, not in a casual and inconsequential way, but the first sentence must be a formal enunciation of a principle. I bought the whole of Dr. Johnson's works at a second-hand bookstore in New York, because, on looking into them, I found his essays appeared to be of solid essay-stuff from beginning to end. I passed by Montaigne's Essays at the same time, because they had a personal and gossipy look. Almost my first literary attempts were moral reflections, somewhat in the Johnsonian style. I lived on the "Rambler" and the "Idler" all one year, and tried to produce something of my own in similar form. As a youth I was a philosopher; as a young man I was an Emersonian; as a middle-aged man I am a literary naturalist; but always have I been an essayist.

It was while I was at school, in my nineteenth year, that I saw my first author; and I distinctly remember with what emotion I gazed upon him, and followed him in the twilight, keeping on the other side of the street. He was of little account, —

a man who had failed as a lawyer, and then had written a history of Poland, which I have never heard of since that time; but to me he was the embodiment of the august spirit of authorship, and I looked upon him with more reverence and enthusiasm than I had ever looked before upon any man. I do not think I could have approached and spoken to him on any consideration. I cannot at this date divine why I should have stood in such worshipful fear and awe of this obscure individual, but I suppose it was the instinctive tribute of a timid and imaginative youth to a power which he was just beginning vaguely to see, — the power of letters.

It was at about this time that I first saw my own thoughts in print, — a communication of some kind to a little country paper published in an adjoining town. In my twenty-second or twenty-third year, I began to send rude and crude essays to the magazines and to certain New York weekly papers, but they came back again pretty promptly. I wrote on such subjects as "Revolutions," "A Man and his Times," "Genius," "Individuality." At this period of my life I was much indebted to Whipple, whose style, as it appears in his earlier essays and in the thin volume of lectures published by Ticknor, Reed & Fields about 1853, is, in my judgment, much better than in his later writings. It was never a good style, not at all magnetic or penetrating, but it was clear and direct, and, to my mind at that period, stimulating. Higginson had just begun to publish his polished essays in the "Atlantic," and I found much help in them also. They were a little cold, but they had the quality which belongs to the work of a man who looks upon literature as a fine art. My mind had already begun to turn to outdoor themes, and Higginson gave me a good send-off in this direction. But the master-enchanter of this period of my life and of many following years was Emerson. While at school, in my nineteenth year, in my search for essays I had carried to my room one volume of his, but I could do nothing with it. What, indeed, could a Johnsonian youth make of Emerson? A year or so later I again opened one of his books in a Chicago bookstore, and was so taken with the first taste of it that I then and there purchased the three volumes, — the "Essays" and the "Miscellanies." All that summer I fed upon them and steeped myself in them: so that when, a year or two afterwards, I wrote an essay on "Expression" and sent it to the "Atlantic," it was so Emersonian that the editor thought some one was trying to palm off on him an early essay of Emerson's which he had not seen. Satisfying himself that Emerson had published no such paper, he printed it in the November number of 1860. It had not much merit. I remember this sentence, which may contain some truth aptly put: "Dr. Johnson's periods act like a lever of the third kind: the power applied always exceeds the weight raised."

It was mainly to break the spell of Emerson's influence and to get upon ground of my own that I took to writing upon outdoor themes. I wrote half a dozen or more sketches upon all sorts of open-air subjects, which were published in the New York "Leader." The woods, the soil, the waters, helped to draw out the pungent Emersonian flavor and restore me to my proper atmosphere. But to this day I am aware that a suggestion of Emerson's manner often crops out in my writings. His mind was the firmer, harder substance, and was bound to leave its mark upon my own. But, in any case, my debt to him is great. He helped me to better literary expression, he quickened my perception of the beautiful, he stimulated and fertilized my religious nature. Unless one is naturally more or less both of a religious and of a poetic turn, the writings of such men as Emerson and Carlyle are mainly lost upon him. Two thirds of the force of these writers, at least, is directed into these channels. It is the quality of their genius, rather than the scope and push of their minds, that endears them to us. They quicken the conscience and stimulate the character as well as correct the taste. They are not the spokesmen of science or of the reason, but of the soul.

About this period I fell in with Thoreau's "Walden," but I am not conscious of any great debt to

Thoreau: I had begun to write upon outdoor themes before his books fell into my hands, but he undoubtedly helped confirm me in my own direction. He was the intellectual child of Emerson, but added a certain crispness and pungency, as of wild roots and herbs, to the urbane philosophy of his great neighbor. But Thoreau had one trait which I always envied him, namely, his indifference to human beings. He seems to have been as insensible to people as he was open and hospitable to nature. It probably gave him more pleasure to open his door to a woodchuck than to a man.

Let me confess that I am too conscious of persons, — feel them too much, defer to them too much, and try too hard to adapt myself to them. Emerson says, "A great man is coming to dine with me: I do not wish to please him, I wish that he should wish to please me." I should be sure to overdo the matter in trying to please the great man: more than that, his presence would probably take away my appetite for my dinner.

In speaking of the men who have influenced me, or to whom I owe the greatest debt, let me finish the list here. I was not born out of time, but in good time. The men I seemed to need most were nearly all my contemporaries; the ideas and influences which address themselves to me the most directly and forcibly have been abundantly current in my time. Hence I owe, or seem to owe, more to contemporary authors than to the men of the past. I have lived in the present time, in the present hour, and have invested myself in the objects nearest at hand. Besides the writers I have mentioned, I am conscious of owing a debt to Whitman, Ruskin, Arnold, Wordsworth, Coleridge, and Tennyson. To Whitman I owe a certain liberalizing influence, as well as a lesson in patriotism which I could have got in the same measure from no other source. Whitman opens the doors, and opens them wide. He pours a flood of human sympathy which sets the whole world afloat. He is a great humanizing power. There is no other personality in literature that gives me such a sense of breadth and magnitude in the purely human and personal qualities. His poems are dominated by a sense of a living, breathing man as no other poems are. This would not recommend them to some readers, but it recommends them to such as I, who value in books perennial human qualities above all things. To put a great personality in poetry is to establish a living fountain of power, where the jaded and exhausted race can refresh and renew itself.

To a man in many ways the opposite of Whitman, who stands for an entirely different, almost antagonistic, order of ideas, — to wit, Matthew Arnold, — I am indebted for a lesson in clear thinking and clean expression such as I have got from no other. Arnold's style is probably the most lucid, the least embarrassed by anything false or foreign, of that of any writer living. His page is as clear as science and as vital and flexible as poetry. Indeed, he affords a notable instance of the cool, impartial scientific spirit wedded to, or working through, the finest poetic delicacy and sensibility.

I have not been deeply touched or moved by any English poet of this century save Wordsworth. Nearly all other poetry of nature is tame and insincere compared with his. But my poetic sympathies are probably pretty narrow. I cannot, for instance, read Robert Browning, except here and there a short poem. The sheer mechanical effort of reading him, of leaping and dodging and turning sharp corners to overtake his meaning, is too much for me. It makes my mental bones ache. It is not that he is so subtile and profound, for he is less in both these respects than Shakespeare, but that he is so abrupt and elliptical and plays such fantastic tricks with syntax. His verse is like a springless wagon on a rough road. He is full of bounce and vigor, but it is of the kind that bruises the flesh and makes one bite his tongue. Swinburne has lilt and flow enough, certainly, and yet I cannot read him. He sickens me from the opposite cause : I am adrift in a sea of melodious words, with never an idea to cling to. There is to me something grewsome and uncanny about Swinburne's poetry, like the clammy and rapidly-growing fungi in nature.

It is not health, but disease; it is not inspiration, but a mortal flux. The "Saturday Review," in noticing my last volume, "Signs and Seasons," intimates that I might have found better specimens of sea-poetry to adorn the chapter called "A Salt Breeze" in Mr. Swinburne than those I have given, and quotes the following stanzas from him as proof: —

"Hardly we saw the high moon hanging,
    Heard hardly through the windy night,
Far waters ringing, low reefs clanging,
    Under wan skies and waste white light.

"With chafe and change of surges chiming,
    The clashing channels rocked and rang
Large music, wave to wild wave timing,
    And all the choral waters sang."

Words, words, words! and all struck with the leprosy of alliteration. Such poetry would turn my blood to water. "Wan skies and waste white light," — are there ever any other skies or any other lights in Swinburne?

But this last is an ill wind which I fear can blow no good to any one. I have lived long enough to know that my own private likes and dislikes do not always turn out to be the decrees of the Eternal. Some writers confirm one and brace him where he stands; others give him a lift forward. I am not aware that more than two American writers have been of the latter service to me, — Emerson and Whitman. Such a spirit as Bryant is confirmatory. I may say the same of Whittier and Longfellow. I owe to these men solace and encouragement, but no new territory.

Still, the influences that shape one's life are often so subtile and remote, and of such small beginning, that it will not do to be too positive about these matters. At any rate, self-analysis is a sort of backhanded work, and one is lucky if he comes at all near the truth.

As such a paper must of necessity be egotistical, let me not flinch in any part of my task on that account.

What little merit my style has is the result of much study and discipline. I have taught myself always to get down to the quick of my mind at once, and not fumble about amid the husks at the surface. Unless one can give the sense of vitality in his pages, no mere verbal brightness or scholarly attainments will save him. In the best writing, every sentence is filled with the writer's living, breathing quality, just as in the perfected honeycomb every cell is filled with honey. But how much empty comb there is even in the best books! I wish to give an account of a bird, or a flower, or of any open-air scene or incident. My whole effort is to see the thing just as it was. I ask myself, "Exactly how did this thing strike my mind? What was prominent? What was subordinated? I have been accused of romancing at times. But it is not true. I set down the thing exactly as it fell out. People say, "I do not see what you do when I take a walk." But for the most part they do, but the fact as it lies there in nature is crude and raw: it needs to be brought out, to be passed through the heart and mind and presented in appropriate words. This humanizes it and gives it an added charm and significance. This, I take it, is what is meant by idealizing and interpreting nature. We do not add to or falsely color the facts: we disentangle them, and invest them with the magic of written words.

To give anything like vitality to one's style, one must divest one's self of any false or accidental or factitious mood or feeling, and get down to his real self, and speak as directly and sincerely as he does about his daily business or affairs, and with as little affectation. One may write from the outside of his mind, as it were, write and write, glibly and learnedly, and make no impression; but when one speaks from real insight and conviction of his own, men are always glad to hear him, whether they agree with him or not. So much writing or speaking is like mere machine-work, as if you turned a crank and the piece or discourse came out. It is not the man's real mind, his real experience. This he does not know how to get at; it has no connection with his speaking or writing faculty. How

rare are real poems, — poems that spring from real
feeling, a real throb of emotion, and not from a
mere surface-itching of the mind for literary expression! The world is full of "rhyming parasites,"
as Milton called them. The great mass of the poetry
of any age is purely artificial, and has no root in
real things. It is a kind of masquerading. The
stock poetic forms are masks behind which the
poetlings hide their real poverty of thought and
feeling. In prose one has no such factitious aids;
here he must stand upon his own merits; he has
not the cloak of Milton or Tennyson, or Spenser,
to hide in.

It is, of course, the young writer who oftenest
fails to speak his real mind, or to speak from any
proper basis of insight and conviction. He is carried away by a fancy, a love of novelty, or an affectation of originality. The strange things, the novel
things, are seldom true. Look for truth under your
feet. To be original, Carlyle said, is to be sincere.
When one is young, how many discoveries he
makes, — real mare's-eggs, which by and by turn
out to be nothing but field-pumpkins!

Men who, like myself, are deficient in self-assertion, or whose personalities are flexible and yielding, make a poor show in politics or business, but
in certain other fields these defects have their
advantages. In action, Renan says, one is weak
by his best qualities, — such, I suppose, as tender-

ness, sympathy, religiousness, — and strong by his poorer, or at least his less attractive, qualities. But in letters the reverse is probably true. How many of us owe our success in this field to qualities which in a measure disqualified us for an active career! A late writer upon Carlyle seeks to demonstrate that the "open secret of his life" was his desire to take a hand in the actual affairs of English politics; but it is quite certain that the traits and gifts which made him such a power in literature — namely, his tremendous imagination and his burdened prophetic conscience — would have stood in his way in dealing with the coarse affairs of this world.

In my own case, what hinders me with the world helps me with impersonal nature. I do not stand in my own light. My will, my personality, offer little resistance: they let the shy, delicate influences pass. I can surrender myself to nature without effort, but am more or less restrained and self-conscious in the presence of my fellows. Bird and beast take to me, and I to them. I can look in the eye of an ugly dog and win him, but with an ugly man I have less success.

I have unmistakably the feminine idiosyncrasy. Perhaps this is the reason that my best and most enthusiastic readers appear to be women. In the genesis of all my books, feeling goes a long way before intellection. What I feel I can express, and only what I feel. If I had run after the birds only to write about them, I never should have written anything that any one would have cared to read. I must write from sympathy and love, or not at all: I have in no sort of measure the gift of the ready writer who can turn his pen to all sorts of themes; or the dramatic, creative gift of the great poets, which enables them to get out of themselves and to present vividly and powerfully things entirely beyond the circle of their own lives and experiences. I go to the woods to enjoy myself, and not to report them; and if I succeed, the expedition may by and by bear fruit at my pen. When a writer of my limited range begins to "make believe," or to go outside of his experience, he betrays himself at once. My success, such as it is, has been in putting my own personal feelings and attractions into subjects of universal interest. I have loved Nature no more than thousands upon thousands of others have, but my aim has been not to tell that love to my reader, but to tell it to the trees and the birds and to let them tell him. I think we all like this indirect way the best. It will not do in literature to compliment Nature and make love to her by open profession and declaration : you must show your love by your deeds or your spirit, and by the sincerity of your service to her.

For my part, I never can interview Nature in the reporter fashion: I must camp and tramp with her to get any good, and what I get I absorb through my emotions rather than consciously gather through my intellect. Hence the act of composition with me is a kind of self-exploration to see what hidden stores my mind holds. If I write upon a favorite author, for instance, I do not give my reader something which lay clearly defined in my mind when I began to write: I give him what I find, after closest scrutiny, in the subconscious regions, — a result as unknown to me as to him when I began to write. The same with outdoor subjects. I come gradually to have a feeling that I want to write upon a given theme, — rain, for instance, or snow, — but what I may have to say upon it is as vague as the background of one of Millet's pictures; my hope is entirely in the feeling or attraction which draws my mind that way; the subject is congenial, it sticks to me; whenever it recurs to me, it awakens as it were a warm personal response.

Perhaps this is the experience of all other writers: their subjects find them, or bring the key to their hidden stores. Great poets, like Milton, however, cast about them and deliberately choose a theme: they are not hampered by their sympathies, nor are they prisoners of their own personalities, like writers who depend upon this pack of unconscious impressions at their back. An experience must lie in my mind a certain time before I can put it on paper, — say from three to six months. If there is anything in it, it will ripen and mellow in that time. I rarely take any notes, and I have a very poor memory, but rely upon the affinity of my mind for a certain order of truths or observations. What is mine will stick to me, and what is not will drop off. When I returned from England after a three months' visit in the summer of 1882, I was conscious of having brought back with me a few observations that I might expand into two or three short essays. But when I began to open my pack, the contents grew so upon my hands that it reached many times the measure I at first proposed. Indeed, when I look back over my seven volumes, I wonder where they have all come from. I am like a boy who at the close of the day looks over his string of fish curiously, not one of which did he know of in the morning, and every one of which came to his hand from depths beyond his ken by luck and skill in fishing. I have often caught my fish when I least expected to, and as often my most determined efforts have been entirely unavailing.

It is a wise injunction, "Know thyself," but how hard to fulfil! This unconscious region in one, this unconscious setting of the currents of his life in certain directions, — how hard to know that! The influences of his family, his race, his times, his environment, are all deeper than the plummet of his self-knowledge can reach. Yet how we admire the ready man, the man who always has complete control of his resources, who can speak the right word instantly! My own wit is always belated. After the crisis is past, the right word or the right sentence is pretty sure to appear and mock me by its tardiness.

There is, no doubt, a great difference in men with reference to this knowledge and command of their own resources. Some writers seem to me to be like those military states wherein every man is numbered, drilled, and equipped, and ready for instant service : the whole male population is a standing army. Then there are men of another type who have no standing army. They are absorbed in mere living, and, when the occasion requires, they have to recruit their ideas slowly from the vague, uncertain masses in the background. Hence they never cut a brilliant figure upon paper, though they may be capable of doing real heartfelt work.

INDEX

INDEX

ACHIEVEMENT and fame, 257-261.
Addison, Joseph, 170.
America, Matthew Arnold's criticism of, 90, 91, 117.
Ancients, science of the, 54-58.
Arnold, Matthew, 75; essentially a critic and filled with the sentiment of culture, 89; his criticism of British civilization, 90, 91, 95, 104-106, 108, 109, 127-130; his criticism of America, 90, 91, 117; compared and contrasted with Carlyle, 93-96, 102; preeminently a critical force, 96; a civilizing and centralizing force, 97-99; a serious and noble man, 99, 100; his published works, 99; his Hellenism, 101-129; a classic writer, 102, 103; his devotion to culture, 103; on poetry, 106-108; on religion and religious worship, 109-115, 136; his advocacy of institutionalism, 115-127; on Benjamin Franklin, 118, 119; on Jeremy Bentham, 119; his admiration of the Catholic Church, 122-127; effect of his teaching, 126-129; as a critic of literature, 129-132, 143; his Celtic Literature, 130; his Translating Homer, 130; on Wordsworth, 130; compared with Sainte-Beuve, 130, 131; his style, 132, 133; consecutiveness of his ideas, 133-136, 148, 149; his commonsense, 135, 136; his wit and humor, 126-139; his Friendship's Garland, 138, 139; his calm, unclouded intelligence, 139, 140; his personal appearance, 141, 142; on Emerson, 141-149, 157, 158, 161, 164-168; on Carlyle, 141-145; 156; on Cardinal Newman, 145; 163; his academic bias, 164; 170; the author's debt to, 270; quotations from, 100-112, 113, 117-125, 128, 136-140, 144, 145, 148, 150, 156.
Arrow-heads, Indian, 18, 40.
Astronomy, ancient, 57.
Audubon, John James, 62.
Autobiography, 263, 264.

Bacon, Francis, 95, 170.
Bentham, Jeremy, 119.
Bible, the, Matthew Arnold on, 110, 111; 126, 127.
Birds, ground-building birds and their nests, 190; length of the song season, 191; evolution of, 210, 211.
Birrell, Augustine, on Dr. Johnson and Carlyle, 213-215, 217, 218.
Blackbird, red-winged. See Starling, red-shouldered.
Bluebird (Sialia sialis), notes of, 42.
Bobolink (Dolichonyx oryzivorus), 190.
Brown, Captain John, 8-10.
Browning, Robert, 78, 155; his involved style, 271.
Bryant, William Cullen, 75, 165, 273.
Bumblebee, 224.
Burns, Robert, 173, 174.
Burroughs, John, early and later associations, 264; begins to write, 265-268; fondness for essays, 265; sees his first author, 265, 266; comes under the influ-

283

INDEX

ence of Emerson's writings, 267, 268; takes to writing outdoor sketches, 268; conscious of persons, 269, 270; his debts to various authors, 269–273; his style, 273, 274; his deficiency in self-assertion and its compensating advantages, 276; must write from sympathy and love, or not at all, 277; act of composition a kind of self-exploration, 277, 278; his knowledge and command of his resources, 280.

Butler, Joseph, his *Analogy between Natural and Revealed Religion*, 101.

Byron, Lord, 75.

Carlyle, Thomas, his debt to science, 85, 86; his *Spiritual Optics*, 85; 89; compared and contrasted with Matthew Arnold, 93–96, 102; 98; Arnold's criticism of, 141–144, 145; an unclassical writer, 142, 143; 151; a great writer, 151; his histories, 152–154, 159, 160; his *Oliver Cromwell*, 153; his *Frederick the Great*, 154, 159; his style, 154–156; his *Life of John Sterling*, 155; his attitude toward happiness, 156; not a typical literary man, 163; 165, 169, 170; his heroic sorrow, 175; his service to his age and country, 176; 182; compared and contrasted with Dr. Johnson, 213–221; his imagination, 215; his despair, 215, 216; 256, 276; quotations from, 92, 93, 170, 175, 176, 218, 229, 230.

Catholicism, Matthew Arnold on, 109, 110, 122–127.

Chewink, *or* towhee (*Pipilo erythrophthalmus*), 190.

Christianity, 104; Matthew Arnold on, 111–115, 136.

Church, the English, Matthew Arnold on, 109; 117. *See* Catholicism, Protestantism, *and* Puritanism.

City, the, 234, 235.

Cock, crowing of the, 32.

Coleridge, Samuel Taylor, 75, 219.

Cowley, Abraham, his essays, 178; a lover of solitude, 240, 241; quotations from, 241.

Culture, Arnold's idea of, 103.

Darwin, Charles, 58, 59; full of the sentiment of science, 62–64; 164, 207, 208.

DeKay, Charles, 77.

De Quincey, Thomas, 193.

Dixon, Hepworth, 137.

Dragon-fly, in Tennyson's poem, 78.

Earth, the, future of, 211, 212. *See* Geology.

Emerson, Ralph Waldo, 6, 7, 11, 14, 29, 37; his attitude toward science, 80–86; 89; his *English Traits*, 95; 98; the most unclassical of poets, 108; 135; Matthew Arnold's criticism of, 141–149, 157, 158, 161, 164–168; an unclassical writer, 142, 143; 151, 154; his lack of continuity as a writer, 157, 158; his *Representative Men*, 158; his *English Traits*, 159; his style, 159, 160; his inspiring message, 161; flavor of character strongest in his writing, 162, 163; the spirit of his work, 163; as a poet, 165–170; his personality, 169; his heroic note, 169–175; his *Titmouse*, 173; his service to his age and country, 176; influence of his writings on the author, 267, 268, 272, 273; quotations from, 59, 81–84, 95, 122, 123, 142, 153, 158, 159, 167; 170–173, 233, 269.

England, 89, 90, 121, 122; some points of difference between her natural history and that of New England and New York, 188–191; things and people larger, heavier, stronger, and coarser than in America, 221–224; vehicles in, 222.

English, the, Emerson on, 95;

284

INDEX

Matthew Arnold on, 89, 90, 95, 104–106, 108, 109, 127–130.

English literature, superior in breadth and heartiness to American, 224–226.

Evolution, geology and, 207–213.

Eye, the spirit of the, 55.

Fame and achievement, 257–261.

Fire, the ancient idea of, 56.

Flicker. See High-hole.

Franklin, Benjamin, 118, 119, 135, 170.

Friend in solitude, a, 241, 242.

Frogs, British, 189.

Geology, Emerson on, 83; evolution and, 207–213.

Gibbon, Edward, quotation from, 193.

God, the nature of, 244–249.

Goethe, 64; his scientific ideas, 67, 73, 113, 120, 145, 151; quotations from, 49, 54, 96, 163, 254, 255.

Goldsmith, Oliver, 257, 258, 261.

Greece. See Hellenism.

Grosbeak, pine (*Pinicola enucleator leucura*), 184.

Hanger, the, 191.

Hawthorne, Nathaniel, 75.

Heat, as a form of motion, 82, 83.

Hebraism, 91, 94, 95, 101, 102.

Hellenism, 91, 94, 95, 101–111, 115–118, 127–130.

Herodotus, his view of the sun, 244.

Higginson, Thomas Wentworth, his essays, 267.

High-hole, *or* flicker (*Colaptes auratus luteus*), notes of, 42.

History, 152, 153.

Hog, 186.

Hoopoe, 184.

Hugo, Victor, his treatment of nature, 194, 205, 206; a great man, 194; his riotous sensationalism, 195–205; his *The Man who Laughs*, 195, 198; his *The Toilers of the Sea*, 195–198; his *Les Misérables*, 197, 205, 206; his *Napo-* leon the Little, 198; his *Bug Jargal*, 199; his *Notre Dame*, 199–204; quotations from, 205, 206.

Humboldt, Baron von, his humanism, 64–66.

Idiot boy, an, 187.

Indian and his daughter, an old, 66.

Individualism, Matthew Arnold opposed to the spirit of, 115–123.

Institutionalism, 115–127.

Irving, Washington, 75, 165.

Johnson, Dr. Samuel, compared and contrasted with Carlyle, 213–221; an "old struggler," 214, 215; his sluggishness, 215–217; his sense of duty, 216; his human frailties, 216, 217; his religion and politics, 217, 218; a greater and more picturesque force personally than intellectually, 218, 219; lives through Boswell, 219, 221; 257; quotations from, 126, 216–219, 220, 221.

Junco, slate-colored. See Snowbird.

Keats, John, 72, 75, 79, 97; quotations from, 79.

Landor, Walter Savage, 75, 134, 135; quotation from, 167.

Lark, grasshopper, 184; notes of, 184.

Linnæus, 79.

Literature, contrasted with science, 50, 51, 57–60; not to be supplanted by science, 51–53, 59–62; in the works of scientists, 61–66; does not keep pace with civilization, 67–69; man alone of perennial interest in, 70; things directly related to our natural lives most interesting to, 70–73; future effect of science on, 73, 74; not incompatible with science, 74; use of science in, 75–87; American possessed of more grace and refinement and

INDEX

INDEX

287

INDEX